# 1 | Case Study

CONSERVATION
OF PHOEBE ANNA
TRAQUAIR MURALS
AT MANSFIELD
TRAQUAIR CENTRE
EDINBURGH

by
Fiona Allardyce
with additional material
by Rosemary Mann

Published by
Historic Scotland

ISBN 978 1 904966 50 0

Historic Scotland
© Crown copyright
Edinburgh 2007

Commissioned by
TECHNICAL
CONSERVATION,
RESEARCH AND
EDUCATION
GROUP

D1438313

## AUTHORS

Fiona Allardyce: free-lance conservator, formerly Senior Conservator with Historic Scotland Conservation Centre

Rosemary Mann: Secretary of Mansfield Traquair Trust

Published by Historic Scotland

ISBN  978 1 904966 50 0

Historic Scotland

© **Crown copyright**

Edinburgh 2007

**Commissioned by**

**Technical Conservation, Research and Education Group**

## ACKNOWLEDGEMENTS

Conservators

1993: Linda Fleming

1995: Ray Hemmett

1999: Fiona Allardyce, Robert Sykes, Lauren Murdoch, Conservation Scientist: Catherine Higgitt

2002: Fiona Allardyce, Ailsa Murray, Gillian Cook (HS Intern)

2003-5: The team of conservators for the restoration of the murals was led by Fiona Allardyce, Senior Conservator with the Historic Scotland Conservation Centre, assisted by Ailsa Murray, Conservator. The three interns appointed through the Historic Scotland Internship Programme were Maeve Woolley, Suzanne Ross and Alexia Willox. HS interns who spent any time on the project were Karen Dundas and Amy Crosman. Free-lance conservators who worked on the project were Brian McLaughlin, Sally Cheyne, Owen Davison, Gillian Cook and Karen Dundas (after completing her internship) and, from abroad: Anca Nicolaescu from Romania, Marta Skowronska from Poland and Maria Johanssen from Sweden. Students included James White, Amanda Mitchell, Ibby Lanfaer and Helen Davies. Volunteers included Julian Watson and Shona Fleming and many others who spent short periods on the project.

Mansfield Traquair Trust. Trustees: Duncan Thomson (Chairman), Muriel Buchanan, Elizabeth Cumming, Jocelyn Cunliffe, John Dick OBE, Isla Duncan, Virginia Holt, Fr Columba Flegg (to 2001), Councillor Margaret McGregor (to 2003), Malcolm Mathieson, Malcolm Murray, Anne-Marie Scott, Dianne Stein; Secretary: Rosemary Mann.

Friends of Mansfield Traquair Centre: Kate Love
SATV: Jenny Sharp and Barry Allsop
and the many funding bodies and individuals who contributed to the rescue and restoration of the building and murals.

Historic Scotland: Ingval Maxwell, Eddie Tait, Robert Martin and Moses Jenkins for assisting in bringing the Murals Project and its associated publication and DVDs into being

# CONTENTS

# LIST OF ILLUSTRATIONS

294. Consolidating the edges of the filling, the previous retouching having been removed, HS

295. Filling prepared with lead white paint, HS

296. Poultices softening over-painting, HS

297. Retouching in progress, HS

298. Noah panel, after conservation, SG

299. Joseph panel, before conservation, 1982 photograph, HS

300. Joseph panel, condition diagram

301. Joseph panel, condition diagram - salt damage

302. Joseph panel, condition diagram - plaster

303. Joseph panel, condition diagram - paint

304. Hole in plaster showing cavity behind paint layer, HS

305. Joseph panel, treatment diagram - plaster

306. Joseph panel, treatment diagram - paint

307. Joseph panel, treatment diagram 2

308. Injecting fresh lime mortar, HS

309. Rubbing the adhesive into the paint surface, HS

310. Cleaning the painting after consolidation, HS

311. Painting after consolidation, cleaning and filling ready for in-painting, HS

312. Blocking in the lost areas in watercolour, HS

313. Building up the tone with varnish paints, HS

314. Left side of Joseph panel after conservation, SG

315. David panel, before conservation, 1982 photograph, RCAHMS

316. David panel, condition diagram

317. Shrunk varnish layer with paint layer showing behind, HS

318. David panel, treatment diagram - paint

319. David panel after conservation, SG

320. Nave north wall, Nativity, Wilderness and Ministry panels, before conservation, 2000 photograph, HS

321. Nave north wall, Last Supper and Ascension panels, before conservation, 1995 photograph, HS

322. Nave north wall, diagram of panels

323. Nativity panel, condition diagram

324. Nativity panel, before conservation with facing tissue over cracks and 1995 cleaning trial, HS

325. Nativity panel, treatment diagram - paint

326. Nativity panel, cleaning relief, HS

327. Nativity panel, during cleaning, HS

328. Nativity panel after conservation, SG

329. Alterations to position of heads, HS

330. Christ in the Wilderness, before conservation, HS

330a Christ in the Wilderness, before conservation, HS

330b Christ in the Wilderness, after conservation, SG

331. Christ in the Wilderness, condition diagram

332. Christ in the Wilderness, treatment diagram - paint

333. Ministry panel, before conservation with facing tissue over areas of weak paint, HS

334. Ministry panel, condition diagram

335. Ministry panel, treatment diagram - paint

336. Cleaning Ministry panel, HS

337. Ministry panel during cleaning, HS

337a Ministry panel during cleaning, HS

337b Ministry panel, after conservation, SG

338. Last Supper, condition diagram

339. Last Supper, treatment diagram - paint

340. Last Supper, treatment diagram 2

341. Salt-damaged paint visible through thinned tissue layer, HS

342. Consolidation in progress, HS

343. Cleaning in progress, HS

344. The Betrayal after consolidation and cleaning and before filling and retouching, HS

345. Last Supper panel after conservation, SG

346. Shadow of ewer visible beneath drinking glass, HS

347. Ascension panel, condition diagram

348. Ascension panel, condition diagram - salt damage

349. Ascension panel, condition diagram - paint

350. Damage caused by damp, 1993 photograph, HS

351. Ascension panel, treatment diagram - paint

352. Ascension panel, treatment diagram 2

353. In-painting in progress, HS

354. Ascension panel after conservation, SG

355. Spandrel panels, 2000 photograph, SG

356. Fragments in east bay, 1995 photograph, HS

357. Removing plaster skim, HS

358. Fragments in organ bay before conservation, HS

359. Silver and gold leaf relief work with outlines of processing figures, HS

360. North aisle, ceiling, west and north walls before conservation, SG

361. North aisle ceiling, bays 22-9, condition diagram

362. North aisle ceiling, bays 15-1, condition diagram

363. Timber affected by rot, HS

364. Fragment of ceiling dislodged during roof repairs, HS

365. Hole in ceiling, HS

366. Flaking paint caused by damp and losses along weak joint between lath-and-plaster and joist, HS

367. North aisle ceiling, bays 22-9, treatment diagram

368. North aisle ceiling, bays 15-1, treatment diagram

369. The back of the fallen fragment during treatment, HS

*Marta Skowronska from Poland (Leonardo Programme Scholar) working on the chancel arch*

# FOREWORD

The murals by Phoebe Anna Traquair at the former Catholic Apostolic Church, Mansfield Place, Edinburgh cover an area of over 500 square metres. Despite being greatly appreciated whilst the Church was in use, the subsequent abandonment of the building, and the inevitable degrees of neglect that followed, led to the deterioration of this unique work of Scottish Art. Through the considerable efforts of the Mansfield Traquair Trust, that process of neglect and decay has been reversed. Working jointly with Historic Scotland, and other funding bodies, the Trust has ensured that the building and its murals have been fully conserved and saved for the future.

The conservation of the Mansfield Place Church murals was one of the largest projects of its kind undertaken in Scotland in recent years and much deliberation and debate went into devising an appropriate way forward.

This built upon a decade of intermittent involvement by Historic Scotland's specialist Conservation Centre staff. In March 1993 a report followed a condition survey and first-aid repairs to consolidate loose plaster and flaking paint, limited to lower levels in the nave. In November 1995 a second report followed a condition survey and first-aid repairs to the rest of the murals, accessed using fixed scaffolding. In July 1999 a reassessment of the earlier findings was prepared in support of the application for grant-aid by the Trust. A programme of environmental monitoring followed. As a result of some roof damage in November 2001, first-aid repair work stabilised the affected area of murals and the previously inaccessible nave spandrel panels were investigated and stabilised.

This sporadic commitment eventually lead to the production of a more comprehensive project plan and an integrated funding package, grant aided by Historic Scotland, in August 2003. The agreed approach involved seconding two specialist staff from Historic Scotland's Conservation Centre. The aim was to undertake the conservation work programme and provide some unique training opportunities at the same time. The foundation for this approach also lay in TCRE's Internship Programme. Here, a variety of specialist training needs had been supported over the years. What was recognised in the Mansfield Place project was the possibility of supporting three Internships in mural conservation, whilst also creating short-term placements for a variety of other students. In the event, Historic Scotland agreed to Fiona Allardyce and Ailsa Murray being seconded to lead the conservation work. To increase the size of the team when that was deemed necessary by the programme, they were supported by private sector conservators at various times during the two year project. In support of this approach it was agreed that the Trust would be responsible for providing welfare facilities as required by

health and safety; for supplying scaffolding and support equipment, and for arranging access to the different parts of the building. The Trust also undertook to liaise with the building tenants to ensure an effective integration with their needs.

Fiona Allardyce prepared the project master plan. This was devised in two parts; planning and implementation. Whilst a range of administrative matters were dealt with during the planning phase, conservation work on the Chapel was also undertaken to ensure that a more accurate measure of work progress against the plan intentions could be determined.

During the implementation stage, the work sequence started with the nave spandrels. It then moved on to the north wall, west gable, south wall, chancel arch and chancel ceiling before finishing in the north aisle. Involving a considerable amount of hands-on work, the intention of utilising the project to provide training opportunities for the three young Intern conservators was fully realised. As the project developed training opportunities for other students also became possible. Training opportunities were developed for other students, and involved over twenty individuals from Scotland, other areas of the United Kingdom and from mainland Europe.

Under the inspiration and leadership of Fiona Allardyce, the Interns and students gained valuable practical expertise in consolidation and restoration techniques, and in the effective management, direction and planning of a large complex conservation project. As a result, the number of conservators capable of dealing with mural conservation projects has been greatly increased whilst, at the same time, the Mansfield Place murals have received the appropriate attention they so badly required. Completing the project within time and budget, the quality of the finished work speaks for itself.

The punctilious project records, and the unique illustrative archive of work in progress, have provided the raw material for this publication and its associated DVDs. Given the innovative nature of the planned approach, the manner in which the work was carried out, and the emerging quality of the results, all involved are to be congratulated in achieving such a remarkable outcome. By presenting the detail of their work in this volume, and the related set of two DVDs, the painstaking nature of their commitment, dedication and application to the task is to be warmly applauded.

**Ingval Maxwell, OBE**
Director
Technical Conservation, Research and Education
Historic Scotland
May 2007

*Phoebe Anna Traquair at work in north aisle, Traquair family copyright*

# SUMMARY

'In the cold, grey north it is sombre art that we are led to look for. Therefore, when in Scotland's capital we turn a corner and find ourselves in the small chapel behind the choir-stalls of the Catholic Apostolic Church in Broughton Street, it is little wonder if we catch our breath at surroundings so rich and so little anticipated.'

So wrote Margaret L Macdonald in 1898 in the Arts and Crafts journal *The Studio* (Bibl 1) when seeing the recently completed murals by Phoebe Anna Traquair in this church at the east end of Edinburgh's New Town (Fig 2). That breathtaking moment has now been restored thanks to the combined efforts of Mansfield Traquair Trust and Historic Scotland.

The murals were executed for the Catholic Apostolic Church, a universalist, ecumenical movement of the 19th century that looked forward to the Second Coming of Christ. The prophetic, charismatic nature of the Church found expression in a unique liturgy with elements derived from both Eastern and Western churches, and a strong emphasis on the prophesies of the Book of Revelation.

In 1872, the Church commissioned Sir Robert Rowand Anderson (1834-1921), regarded as the foremost architect in Scotland in the late 19th century, to design a building in Edinburgh suited to their distinctive form of worship. The church was enhanced by a vast scheme of mural decoration, carried out between 1893 and 1901 by Phoebe Anna Traquair (1852-1936), a leading member of the Arts & Crafts movement in Britain. The murals cover 500m$^2$ of the walls and ceilings of the church and the Herculean labour by the artist, the brilliant colour and the soaring space have led to the building being called 'Edinburgh's Sistine Chapel'.

The congregation moved out in 1958 and during the following forty years of disuse or abuse, the building suffered from neglect and lack of maintenance. Water entered the building from poorly maintained gutters and ran down the walls. This caused damage to the murals exacerbated by a century of dirt and grime and deposits left by invasive pigeons.

Mansfield Traquair Trust was founded in 1993 with the aim of finding a viable use for the building and securing its restoration and preservation for the benefit of the public at large. Starting out with nothing but determination and goodwill, the Trust managed to find a use for the building, assemble a funding package and buy the building. This would not have been possible without the encouragement of Historic Scotland, the support of the newly created Heritage Lottery Fund and the assistance of the City of Edinburgh Council which used its powers to stop the building falling into terminal decay and helped to resolve the ownership problem.

From 2000-02 the Trust undertook the repair and conversion of the building into a new headquarters for the Scottish Council for Voluntary Organisations, the umbrella organisation for the voluntary sector in Scotland. Then, once the building had adjusted to being warm and dry, the mammoth task of the restoration of the murals was undertaken. The restoration was carried out by an innovative partnership between the Trust and Historic Scotland combining the restoration of the murals with training and work experience for young conservators. The effect seen by Margaret L Macdonald has been restored and once again *'the whole Chapel scintillates and glows like a jewelled crown'*.

*Above, left to right: Brian McLaughlin, Ibby Lanfaer, Maeve Woolley, Suzanne Ross, Fiona Allardyce, Ailsa Murray*

1.   *The conservation team, HS*

*Below: left to right: Brian McLaughlin, Fiona Allardyce, Ailsa Murray, Marta Skowronska, Amanda Mitchell, Suzanne Ross, Karen Dundas, Maeve Woolley, Julian Watson*

# INTRODUCTION

This report gives an account of the conservation of the mural paintings by Phoebe Anna Traquair in the former Catholic Apostolic Church in Mansfield Place, Edinburgh. It must be stressed, however, that the conservation of the paintings was part of a project to restore and regenerate the entire building and ensure that it had a viable future.

A project of this nature involves many people and groups of people performing a wide range of activities. The eventual refurbishment of first the building, followed by the conservation of the murals were the evident culmination of much of this activity.

Within this document is drawn together information that was gathered over a long period of time, and which took the form of several shorter reports and numerous discussions, which in turn led to decisions being made. Many of the difficulties and hitches that inevitably occur whilst undertaking such a massive project are, of course, not included, and, I hope that the report will read as a continuous sequence of events. However, it is important to state that difficulties did occur, and that nothing is as simple as it looks when it has all been neatly summarised and wrapped up!

The report is accompanied by a DVD made up of film footage taken while the conservation project was underway. This complements the report and provides a better record of the people and processes involved than can possibly be given by a written document.

In several of the images within the report and the accompanying DVD it may be noted that the conservators are frequently working without hard hats or respirators. Following discussions with the Health and Safety advisors for the project it was agreed that wearing hard hats would cause a greater rather than a reduced hazard both to the conservators and the paintings. The hats restrict and inhibit movement, particularly in constricted areas, thus reducing safety and awareness. Since the site was no longer a building site, it was decided that hard hats need only be worn when working directly beneath someone. The use of toxic solvents was kept to a minimum, thus allowing the conservators to undertake several treatments without needing to use respirators. Fume extractors were employed to extract toxic fumes where necessary so that respirators were only required when using certain chemicals for prolonged periods of time.

2.    *The Awakening, panel in chapel, MTT*

3.    *Mansfield Traquair Centre, chancel arch, SG*

# 1 THE BUILDING

## 1.1 The Catholic Apostolic Church

The former Catholic Apostolic Church, now called the Mansfield Traquair Centre, is a Category A listed building in Mansfield Place, Edinburgh (Midlothian, OS Reference: NT 257 747) within the Edinburgh New Town Conservation Area.

The church (Fig 4) was built between 1873-1894 by Sir Robert Rowand Anderson to provide a new, and considerably larger place of worship for the rapidly expanding Edinburgh congregation of the Catholic Apostolic Movement. The congregation's previous church was a small building (still standing) in Broughton Street.

The Catholic Apostolic movement was formally established in 1835. Its growth in Scotland in the 1820s was due to the charismatic and influential preacher and theologian Edward Irving, but the more developed movement was part of a world wide group of congregations. One of the most striking doctrines of the movement was its belief in the second coming of Christ at the end of the millennium preceded by the apocalyptic battle of Armageddon (expected in the late 1860s).

The movement quickly gained popularity and twelve new Apostles were appointed to organise congregations around the world, each with an elaborate hierarchy of clergy (angels, priests and deacons). The worship by these congregations combined elements of Catholic, Anglican and Eastern Orthodox liturgy with great emphasis on ritual and music.

Although the Apocalypse did not occur as predicted, the Edinburgh congregation continued to flourish during the later 19th century and was clearly confident and well enough endowed to commission an expensive new church. The congregation included wealthy and respected members of society – the Angel at that time was a Writer to the Signet and the Archdeacon (who supervised the commission of the paintings) became the Lord Justice Clerk.

4.   *Mansfield Traquair Centre, early view of exterior, Philip van den Berg*

3

5.  *View of interior, taken after 1894 (chancel arch murals complete) and before 1898 (nave panels undecorated), probably 1896/7 (scaffolding in north aisle), Philip van den Berg*

Because events failed to develop as expected, it was inevitable that the Catholic Apostolic movement could not survive in the form in which it began. By common agreement the decision was made not to replace those Apostles who died and all ordinations ceased on the death of the last Apostle in 1901. This guaranteed the eventual demise of the various churches since the Apostles alone had authority to ordain angels and priests.

The last angel died in 1960 and the last priest in 1971. One by one the buildings which were maintained by the London-based trustees and locally cared for by the deacons were closed; the church in Mansfield Place in 1958 following the death of the priest.

### 1.2 The Building of the Church

The architectural requirements of the congregation were very precise and these were specified in the competition brief won by Sir Robert Rowand Anderson. The architectural style was to be Norman. The requirements included: a free standing altar visible to all present; a sanctuary large enough to accommodate the numerous clergy and a nave arranged so that the congregation could sit, kneel, circulate and easily see the colourful processions and ceremonies (Fig 5).

The foundation stone was laid in November 1873, the ceremony attended by two thousand people. The nave, chancel and clergy house were first to be built, and were consecrated in 1876. Eight years later, between 1884–6, the narthex and baptistery were added. Anderson's involvement with the building continued until 1894 when the elaborate baldacchino over the altar was built to his design, with sculpture by W Birnie Rhind (Figs 6, 7 & 8).

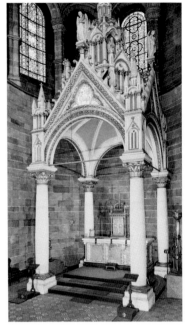

*6.    Baldacchino with altar and tabernacle,
RCAHMS*

1. Narthex
2. Baptistery
3. West Wall
4. Nave
5. Chancel Arch
6. South Chapel
7. North Aisle
8. Baldacchino
9. Organ Case

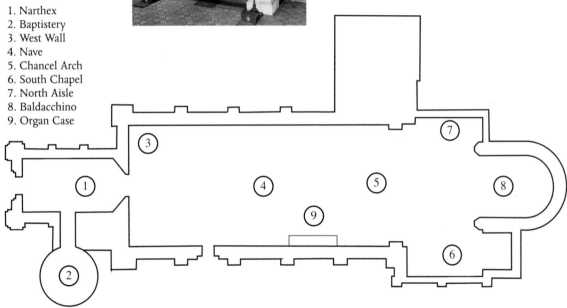

*7.    Plan of building, Simpson and Brown Architects*

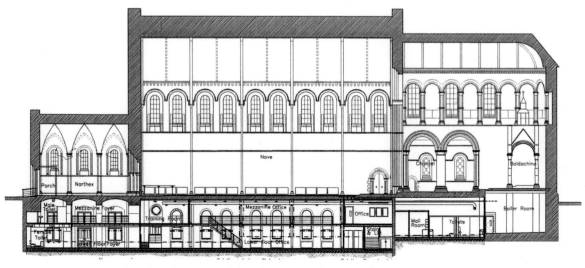

*8.    West-East Section through narthex, nave and chancel, Simpson and Brown Architects*

The nave measures 33.5m long, 13.5m wide and 18m high. It is of five bays, aisleless, with a barrel vaulted ceiling and a stair tower at each corner. It is lit by five pairs of clerestory windows (with plain leaded glass) on each side and by a wheel window (stained glass) in the west wall.

The east wall of the nave is pierced by an immense chancel arch, leading to a deep chancel and apse. On either side of the chancel there is a chapel to the south and a small side aisle to the north. Both may be entered from the nave, but are also connected to the chancel by open arcades. The chapel (Fig 10) measures approximately 9.5m long by 5.5m wide and has a barrel vault and two stained glass windows. The chapel has a slightly narrower chancel at its east end, which measures approximately 4m wide by 2.5m long with a stone altar and a three-light stained glass window. The north aisle (Fig 11) is approximately 9.5m long by 2m wide, with a pitched roof and three stained glass windows. The chapel was used for regular weekday services, whereas the smaller north aisle was less frequently used.

## 1.3 Stained Glass

The stained glass in the chancel (except the east window), chapel and north aisle is by Hardman Studios of Birmingham. *The Hardman Catalogue of Windows* (Bibl 2) shows that *The Transfiguration*, first made in 1848, was lengthened by two feet by the firm in 1876 for installation in the east window of the chapel (Fig 9). The initial order came from T G Dickson of 34 York Place, Edinburgh, so this window is most likely to be a translation from the earlier Edinburgh church building which has an apse window of the same dimensions. Hardman only started making stained glass in 1845 and this was therefore an early piece. The other Hardman windows date from 1876 and 1877. The wheel window in the nave, the east window in the chancel and the west window in the narthex are by Ballantine and were installed in 1885 (Bibl 3). The windows in the baptistery (dated 1905) are also attributed to Ballantine (Bibl 4).

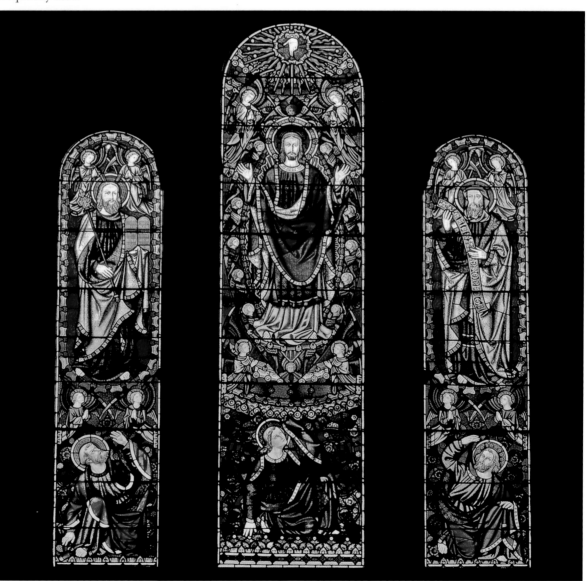

9. *East window of chapel, SG*

10.  *View of chapel showing west wall and ceiling, SG*

11.  *View from north aisle to nave, SG*

*12. Sketch by Robert Rowand Anderson showing intended decoration, The Builder, 6 Jan 1883, RCAHMS*

# 2 THE MURALS

## 2.1 The Requirements of the Congregation

In addition to a precise architectural brief, the Edinburgh congregation added an unusual request for elaborate mural decoration consisting of apocalyptic scenes on the chancel arch and west gable and biblical scenes on the north and south wall. A preliminary sketch of the interior by Anderson (Fig 12) indicates that all surfaces in the nave, including the ceiling, were to be painted but in the event the decoration was restricted to the walls.

The murals eventually painted by Phoebe Anna Traquair decorate the chancel arch and west wall from 5m above floor level to the ceiling and fill a row of 2m by 5m panels on the nave walls below the clerestory windows. The nave walls above the clerestory windows to the cornice (spandrel panels) were also painted.

The walls and ceilings of both the chapel and north aisle were painted, but there is no mural decoration in the narthex or the baptistery.

## 2.2 Earlier Decorative Schemes

During an inspection of the church in 1999 remains of a stylised stencilled dado band were observed on the lower walls of the nave that lie below the painted panels (Figs 13 & 14). Cross section samples of the paint layers on the lower walls revealed two simple stencil decorations overlying one another. The second scheme extended up the wall beyond the level of the dado. It was a pale red design on a darker red ground with gilded details (Fig 15). Study of the wall in raking light suggests that both these schemes survive all around the nave walls, but their condition is not known. Sometime between 1923-42, these lower panels were painted steel-grey (Bibl 5) (see Fig 13).

The upper panels in the nave (to be painted later by Phoebe Anna Traquair), were known to have been plastered and decorated with a simple red line border, about 5 cm wide, set at about 20 cm from the edge. This line may still be seen on the wall that is now hidden by the organ case, and must have been clearly visible before the organ was erected on the south wall of the nave in 1895, two years before the artist started work in the nave (Fig 16). The red line survives on the other panels beneath the later decoration by Phoebe Anna Traquair, and may be clearly seen in raking light (see Fig 83).

The pink tone of the plaster (which now lies beneath Traquair's paler preparation layer) may indicate that the red line is linked with the maroon and pink stencilled scheme found on the lower wall surface of the nave.

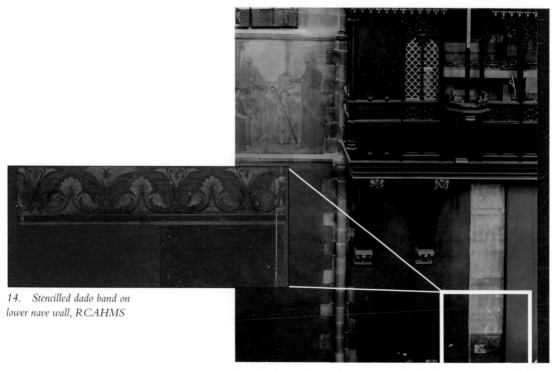

14. *Stencilled dado band on lower nave wall, RCAHMS*

13. *South wall of nave showing traces of earlier decorative schemes, MTT*

9

*15.  Stencilled decoration on lower nave wall, RCAHMS*

*16.  Red line border on panel behind organ case, HS*

It is possible that the decoration of the chancel ceiling (Fig 17) belongs with these earlier schemes. But evidence, including early photographs, that might support this theory is far from conclusive and the exact place of the ceiling decoration within the sequence of events is unknown.

During preliminary research, cross sections were taken from the various doors to see what the original colours were, and if there was any variation between doors according to their liturgical use. The results were a little inconclusive. The south and east doors appear to have been red originally. However, a thin white ground was found beneath the red paint on the north door. This may be interpreted as a ground coat, or could indicate that

this door was painted white, although this seems unlikely. We know that the doors were painted in red during a bout of cleaning and repainting at some stage between 1923 and 1942 which is recorded in a letter from Dr RF Stevenson (Bibl 5), and since no earlier colour was found it is likely that they were always painted red.

The organ pipes were removed after the Catholic Apostolic congregation left the church but the wooden case survives (see Figs 5 & 13). The wood surface is stained a reddish colour and then varnished. The varnish appears to have darkened considerably, and probably the woodwork would have originally appeared a lighter colour. The gilding on the mouldings at the edges of the supporting buttresses of the organ goes over the red stain.

*17.  Chancel ceiling, SG*

*18. Detail of organ case, SG*

The gilding on the tracery within the arches on the front of the organ case is applied directly onto the prepared wood (Fig 18).

It may be that the finishes on the organ case have been restored at some stage, with the dark varnish and the gilding on the buttresses added later, but this is difficult to verify. Early photographs show very clearly how the gilded edges of the large timber ribs of the barrel vaulted ceiling of the nave catch the light. The timber has a dark reddish colour, and the organ case would have sat well within this colour scheme. The gilding on the ribs has now dulled and become dirty, and this strong design element created by the gilded bands, which accentuate the shape of the ceiling is somewhat reduced (see Fig 5).

It would seem therefore, that before the main commission began, the interior had one or two simple painted schemes whose predominant colour scheme was pink, red and gold. The interior would have seemed quite light and pleasant, but completely different from the intensely colourful and powerful decoration that was to follow.

## 2.3 The Commission

The commission both of the architecture and the paintings was headed by J H A Macdonald who later became Lord Justice Clerk. He was a deeply learned theologian and guided the work closely, specifying the subject matter and approving the artist's proposals. He shared the belief of both the artist herself, and the Edinburgh Social Union who were instrumental in commissioning of the work that the *'arts express ideas and feelings as powerful as words can do'*.

Phoebe Anna Traquair (1852-1936) (see photograph page xiv) occupies a unique position within British Art. She was Scotland's first woman artist of the modern age

and a valued contributor to the British Arts & Crafts Movement, working in such diverse fields as embroidery, leather tooling and bookbinding, manuscript illumination, enamelwork, furniture decoration, easel painting and mural decoration. The decoration of the Catholic Apostolic Church in Edinburgh, her first professional commission, helped to confirm this reputation.

The choice of artist to undertake this immense commission seems to have gone back to discussions by the executive committee of the Edinburgh Social Union following the success of the Song School decoration. The Union raised the suggestion of sponsoring a second Traquair scheme, and proposed both the new Catholic Apostolic Church and the Portrait Gallery as possible sites (both Anderson buildings). The artist herself was decidedly more interested in painting religious subjects, and the proposal that she should paint the Catholic Apostolic church was carried from meeting to meeting, and eventually, after some indecision, the commission was awarded.

Having seen the building, Phoebe Anna Traquair was determined to paint its walls; A F Morris reported in 1905 (Bibl 6): *'Music has had a great influence on Mrs Traquair's career. Especially it has played its part in her mural designs; it was indeed the prime factor in the decoration of the Catholic and Apostolic Cathedral of Edinburgh, for, straying into the new building one day while service was in progress, the swelling notes of the organ resounding through the church so worked upon her, that when the prayers were over she walked up to one of the Deacons and, without pause or ceremony, assailed him with the remark "I want to paint these walls". Being well known, her demand met with courteous if amused attention, and a slight discussion as to money and other difficulties ensued, which she concluded by saying: "Well! If I am to paint these walls, no one in Edinburgh can prevent me; and if I am not going to paint them, no one in Edinburgh can make me!"'*

*19. Chancel arch, SG*

## 2.4 Iconography

As noted above, the iconography decided by the representatives of the Catholic Apostolic Church reflected the core beliefs of the church. (Biblical references are given in the Appendices.)

### 2.4.1 Chancel Arch (east wall)

The wall surface of the chancel arch (Fig 19) is divided horizontally by several stone mouldings or string courses. Within the panels thus formed the artist painted an interpretation of the visionary descriptions of The Worship of Heaven from the Book of Revelation. This illustrates the special apocalyptic symbolism of the Catholic Apostolic church.

In the lowest panels are the four holy beasts: each had six wings and the heads respectively of a man, a lion, an eagle and an ox. Above each symbolic image are four winged cherubim representing the four orders of the Catholic Apostolic ministry.

Above these are choirs of angels and trumpeting angels. Next are the twenty-four enthroned elders and above the *'sea of glass mingled with fire'* is *'the great multitude that no man can number'*. A transparent rainbow traverses the four cherubim and has the effect of focusing the design on the tabernacle on the altar in which the sacrament was reserved.

*20. Chapel, Annunciation with image of Leaderfoot viaduct, SG*

21.  *Chapel chancel ceiling, south side, SG*

### 2.4.2 Chapel and North Aisle

In both the chapel and north aisle is illustrated the parable of the wise and foolish virgins as an allegory of the journey of the human spirit through life. The parable begins in the chapel and continues in the north aisle. Below the narrative scenes is a highly decorated dado band with medallions containing scenes that have a symbolic connection to the narrative above. On the west wall beneath the virgins as they set off on their journey is a particularly beautiful image of the Annunciation, the symbolic beginning of new life, set in the Scottish borders, with the Leaderfoot viaduct in the background (Fig 20). On the south wall, beneath the sleeping virgins being awoken are medallions of Christ with the sleeping Disciples, the three Marys at the tomb and the Entombment, symbolising spiritual awakening in life and death.

The arch separating the chapel from its chancel shows the feet of Christ ascending into heaven flanked by a dove to the left and a serpent to the right. Angels and more foliation decorate the soffits of the arches between the chapel and the main chancel. The chapel ceiling illustrates the Garden of Heaven and the chancel ceiling is decorated with six red-winged seraphim in front of horizontal bands illustrating six verses from Psalm 148 representing the six days of creation (Fig 21). Above the arch leading into the nave is Christ and the Traveller.

The final three scenes of the parable are in the north aisle with the climax in the centre panel where the wise virgins are greeted by the hands of Christ reaching through an

22.  *Decoration of spandrel panels, Mansfield Traquair Trust, in RCAHMS*

23.  *North aisle, centre panel, SG*

open doorway representing the union of human with divine spirits (Fig 23). Above and below are vignettes in a rich foliated border with flowers, mythical beasts, birds, and a parade of animals reflecting the Creation. The central medallion beneath the main scene where the wise virgins are received shows a spirit kneeling before the Eucharist – the consummation of the human with the divine. The north wall may be a homage to William Morris who died in 1896, the year before the north aisle was painted. The ceiling is stylistically based on 17th century Scottish painted ceilings. Above the arch into the nave is a reference to *The Light of the World* by William Holman Hunt, personally known to Traquair since the late 1880s.

### 2.4.3 Nave North and South Walls

The north wall of the nave is painted with scenes from the Life of Christ; on the south wall are the corresponding Old Testament precursors. The north wall panels represent the Nativity, Christ in the Wilderness, Christ's Ministry, Last Supper and Resurrection; the south wall panels Adam and Eve, Noah, the story of Joseph and the story of Solomn and David. It is notable that the Passion is absent from the north wall, reflecting the paramount importance of the Resurrection and After-Life for the Catholic Apostolic Church. In the spandrel panels above the windows was what appears from old photographs to have been a procession of angels set within a garden (Fig 23).

### 2.4.4 West Wall

The west wall (Fig 24) would have faced the congregation as they left the church, providing them with an uplifting vision to carry with them through the day. The main, upper, part of the wall illustrates the second coming of Christ. Christ receives the worship of all creation and dispenses the grace and blessing of Almighty God; risen souls are greeted by ministering angels and a heavenly choir sing and play on harps and trumpets. Within the highly decorated frieze beneath the principal scene are three medallions. The central medallion contains a depiction of the Pentecost. Elizabeth Cumming has suggested the female figure in pink in the foreground may be a self-portrait of Phoebe Anna Traquair as Mary Magdalene (Fig 25). The medallion on the left shows a new heart being given to the people, that on the right a figure being relieved of its burden. The background shows, on the left, the Tree of Life with the Dove of the Holy Spirit and sheep and, on the right, the Tree of Knowledge with the Serpent and goats. The inclusion of this frieze within the overall conception of the west wall links this wall firmly to the decoration of the chapel and north aisle. The stylistic link encourages the viewer to grasp fully the connection of the second coming with the significance of the narrative of the wise and foolish virgins. It also may have had a more personal resonance with the artist's own belief in the progress of the soul.

### 2.4.5 Chancel ceiling

As noted above, it is not possible to know whether or not the chancel ceiling (see Fig 17) belongs within the Traquair scheme, or is part of the earlier decoration. The ceiling was painted by the firm of Andrew Hutton (he was a deacon of the Catholic Apostolic Church). Other than this we have no information about this part of the decoration, although Elizabeth Cumming thinks the blue central panel is based on a design by Traquair. The design centres around a tree form (Fig 26), possibly an orange tree (the sin apple?) set against bands of different colours. A possible interpretation of the design is to see

24. *West wall, SG*

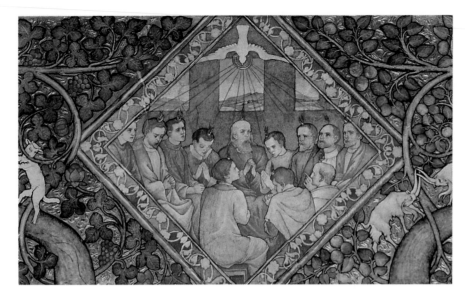

*25. Pentecost medallion, SG*

the tree as being set against four zones; water, earth, air (or sky) and heaven. The transition from one zone to the next is marked by wide paper strips tacked to the wooden ceiling, the lower paper strip has the roots of the trees painted over it and may represent the earth. Air is separated from heaven by a narrower paper strip. Most of the paintwork has been applied as a stencil, with some finishing off done free-hand. A study of the Robert Rowand Anderson sketch of the interior (Fig 12) shows some of the features eventually painted on the chancel and the nave ceilings.

### 2.5 Order of Work

There are no surviving documents relating to the painting of the church (e.g. bills, receipts etc). The following information is based upon passing references made by Phoebe Anna Traquair in letters to her nephew Willie Moss (Bibl 7), written during the years that she was working in the church, and the evidence of dated signatures or monograms within the decoration (listed in the Appendices). The latter are more numerous at first, particularly in the chapel, but become increasingly rare as the artist progressed with the scheme.

Traquair began in the autumn of 1893 with the great chancel arch (Fig 27). During conservation, sufficient evidence emerged to substantiate the conclusion that the lower panels were painted first, and the upper parts followed. She completed the chancel arch after about eighteen months in 1895.

From here Traquair proceeded in January 1896 into the chapel where there are six dated signatures or monograms (Fig 28). She began in January and by March had reached the scene of the ten sleeping virgins. She worked through the summer and autumn on the chapel and during the later autumn moved into the north aisle. In both the chapel and north aisle she completed the walls before beginning work on the ceilings. The north aisle was completed by early 1897.

There is less information about the nave. Traquair worked on the life of Christ on the north wall first. By February 1898 she was finishing the 'second large panel in the nave', and completed this wall by May 1898. The signature and date 1898 in lower right-hand corner of Ascension panel might indicate that this was the last panel that she painted on this wall. It took about 3-4 months to complete the north nave wall – which means she worked at a rate of more than one panel a month.

The panels on the south wall were then painted. The precise date is not known, but they must have been completed by about 1899.

It is not known when Traquair painted the spandrel panels above the clerestory windows of the north and south walls of the nave.

The west wall was painted last, starting at the top with the Second Coming and finishing with the lower decorative band. Traquair mentions working on this border in October 1901. All the decoration was completed by the end of 1901.

The speed with which the painting was done is notable – just over eight years to complete the entire decoration. The preparation of the walls was carried out by the firm of Andrew Hutton. This would have included plastering and the application of the priming coat (described below).

The only part of the painting with which Traquair is known to have had help was the upper reaches of the chancel wall where John Fraser Matthew, an assistant of the architect Robert Lorimer, was briefly assigned to her from 1893. The bulk of the work was done by Traquair alone.

### 2.6 Historical and Art Historical Importance of the Decoration

The decoration of the church is the last of three important surviving interiors by Phoebe Anna Traquair

26. *Chancel ceiling (during conservation) showing tree form, SG*

27. *View taken from nave clerestory into chancel after 1894 (chancel arch murals complete) but before 1896/7 (north aisle without decoration), Mansfield Traquair Trust*

in Edinburgh; the others being the Mortuary of the Hospital for Sick Children (1885-6 and 1896-8) (Fig 29) and St Mary's Cathedral Song School (1888-92) (Fig 30). The Catholic Apostolic Church is the largest of these commissions and shows Traquair at her peak in terms of technique and mastery of the art of large scale mural decoration.

Phoebe Anna Traquair was not a member of the Catholic Apostolic congregation but she respected their beliefs and instilled the decoration with her own faith and imagination. She threw herself wholeheartedly into the commission with her characteristic thoughtfulness and honesty and this shines through the paintings and gives the interior a great intensity of religious feeling.

However, the importance of the decoration in Mansfield Place Church lies not only in its aesthetic appeal and religious significance but also in its place in the wider Edinburgh and British context. Traquair was a member of the Edinburgh Social Union (mentioned above); a group of artists and thinkers founded in the 1880s by the botanist Patrick Geddes and like-minded local philanthropists. The aims of the Union were many, but included the belief that art could inspire and enlighten and that mural painting was an essential adornment of public buildings of all kinds.

The paintings at Mansfield Place Church as much as fulfilling the requirements of the Catholic Apostolic congregation are a survival of this philosophy which marked a revival of mural painting in Scotland.

Traquair herself was not exclusively a mural painter but worked in a wide range of media, on both large and small scales, and was seen by her contemporaries to be an important figure in the Arts and Crafts movement.

Although in the 20th century the paintings were not valued as highly as they should have been, more recently they, and the artist, have been the subject of serious art historical study, particularly by Dr Elizabeth Cumming who made the artist the subject of her unpublished PhD thesis *Phoebe Anna Traquair and her contribution to Arts and Crafts in Edinburgh* of 1986 and who published *Phoebe Anna Traquair 1852–1936* in 2005 (see Bibliography).

28. *Phoebe Anna Traquair monogram and date in chapel, HS*

29. *Mortuary, Royal Hospital for Sick Children, Elizabeth Cumming, RHSC W & N walls*

30. *St Mary's Cathedral Song School, HS*

# 3 DECLINE AND RESCUE

## 3.1 Decline

The survival of a scheme of mural painting is dependent largely upon the fortunes of the building in which it is painted, and this decoration is no exception. It seems that the building itself had some design features which led to damp entering at the wall head of the nave and within the first two decades after the paintings were completed in 1901 several problems had developed that required remedial treatment. According to Dr Stevenson (Bibl 5) whose father was the 5th Angel (1919-1923) 'Phoebe Traquair was often seen on the scaffolding repairing the paintings'.

In 1910 Traquair had to return to make repairs to the painting in the spandrel panels at the top of the nave walls, which by 1926 had all but completely disappeared. And, although not recorded, Traquair returned to replaster and repaint a large section of the Doubting Thomas vignette in the chapel, which she signed and dated 1924 (Fig 31).

31. *Doubting Thomas medallion, SG (see fig 159 for extent of repair)*

Dr Stevenson also noted that some time between 1923-42: *'a comprehensive cleaning was carried out with scaffolding everywhere and dripping with water and a mild soap. Mr Soeder (Senior) of Dobie & Son, George Street, was in charge, supervised by James Simpson, a youngish deacon ... All the Traquair work was cleaned, revealing bright colours, while to set these off the blotched untidy plaster below was coated with Dobie's well known textured undercoat and matt painted in grey. All the doors were three coated in cardinal red ... Some are now repainted brown and the painted work has dulled again, but at the time the freshened building was a delight'.*

We cannot tell from this what the cleaning agent was, or if the paintings were revarnished.

It is interesting to note that cleaning was considered quite a normal procedure. In 1901 the Song School murals were *'cleaned under the direction of the artist and the colours were found as fast and crisp as the day on which they were put on'* (Bibl 8).

Significant settlement cracks had formed, presumably quite early on, on the west wall (Fig 32), over the door in the south wall of the nave and over the windows in the north aisle. These were filled and retouched, it is not known precisely when or by whom, but possibly during the general cleaning of the paintings mentioned above some time between 1923 and 1942 (Fig 33). The plastering and repainting of these cracks was done quite sympathetically, but did not look like the work of Traquair. The painting technique appeared to be conventional oil paint (with no addition of beeswax) and the varnish was not soluble in industrial methylated spirits (IMS), but slightly soluble in acetone. The area fluoresced very darkly in UV light indicating a different medium (possibly pure oil paint).

32. *Crack in west wall, SG*

*33. Repainting at crack over south door, RCAHMS*

For several decades after this first wave of events, the paintings apparently remained relatively stable. However, following the departure of the Catholic Apostolic congregation in 1958, the building was left unused or underused and consequently maintained in a piecemeal and unsatisfactory way with intermittent heating and minimal structural repairs (Bibl 5).

The church stood empty from 1958 until it was taken over by the Reformed Baptist Church, to whom it was sold in 1974. Initially the nave was used for worship, then only the narthex, at which time the church furniture (stalls, organ pipes, font etc) were disposed of so the nave could be used as a warehouse (Fig 34). The Baptist congregation maintained the building until the early 1980s. In 1988 the church was sold to a property developer who obtained consent for conversion of the building into offices (including a free-standing structure in the nave which would have blocked the view of the murals) but the scheme was never implemented. During the 1990s the church was a night club and entertainment venue 'Cafe Graffiti', with performances held in the main church but most activity being in the basement rooms.

*34. Building in use as a warehouse, RCAHMS, copyright Joe Rock*

Eventually such long-term lack of maintenance of the building led to a noticeable deterioration in the condition of the paintings. Failing rainwater goods resulted in water getting into the building along wall-heads, string courses and from valley gutters. In several instances, notably in the chapel, water was running over the paintings (Fig 35). Salts were crystallising on and beneath the paint layer, making it and the plaster fall off or become weak.

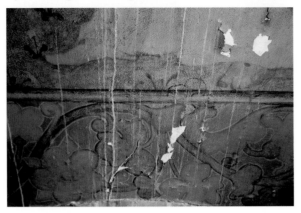

*35. Water damage in chapel, HS*

The damp had also affected the relief and gilded work, for example the halo of the ox on the chancel arch had been completely lost (Fig 36). However, in some instances these had become weak and brittle as much because of the way they had been made originally (see below).

*36. Loss of relief work, HS*

Growing awareness of the importance of the work of Phoebe Anna Traquair and local concern over proposals for uses unsympathetic to the building and detrimental to the amenity of the area led to the formation of the community based Friends of Mansfield Place Church in 1992 and, to turn aspiration into action, the Mansfield Traquair Trust in 1993. The objectives of the Trust were to rescue the building from unsympathetic ownership, find an appropriate and viable use for the building, restore and convert the building, restore the murals and ensure that the building was maintained for future generations.

### 3.2 The Role of the City Council and Historic Scotland in the Rescue

Mansfield Place Church (as it was then known) came to public prominence in 1993 when it was open to complement the exhibition on Phoebe Anna Traquair in the Scottish National Portrait Gallery. By this time, the City of Edinburgh Council had been concerned for several years at the deterioration of the building.

The City Council used its powers to undertake emergency repairs in 1993 to stop the worst of the leaks and commissioned Historic Scotland to undertake a condition survey and emergency stabilisation work to the murals which were carried out in 1993 and 1995. By these actions, the rate of deterioration of the building was slowed and the murals were held on the walls, giving the City Council and Mansfield Traquair Trust time to resolve the ownership problem.

In addition to the basic stabilisation work, staff of the Historic Scotland Conservation Centre (HSCC) wrote a series of reports which document the condition of the paintings through the 1990s.

The earliest report dates from 1993 and was based upon observations made from a hydraulic hoist, thus access was limited. It did not cover the paintings in the side chapels. The report included research into contemporary accounts of the artist's technique, information about previous restorations of the decoration and a brief description of the then condition of the murals. Protective facings of Eltoline tissue (acid-free long-fibre manilla tissue) were applied to weak areas using a gelatine solution (Fig 37) and cleaning trials were made. Broad recommendations for treatment were proposed. The report contained many useful photographs showing the condition of some of the damaged areas before facings were applied.

The second report was written in 1995. A fixed scaffolding had been constructed to allow emergency first aid treatment which provided access to inspect the upper parts of the gable walls as well as the north and south walls of the nave and the two side chapels. Further protective tissue was applied where necessary, and particularly vulnerable flaking paint was secured with polyvinyl acetate (PVA) (Fig 38). Isolated areas of loose plaster were also secured with lime/PVA mix. The report included a condition survey and assessment of damage

37.  *Pentecost panel with facing tissue, SG*

38.  *Conservator securing flaking paint on chancel arch, HS*

since 1993, with many photographs showing damaged areas before and after facing and first aid treatment.

The third report dates from 1999 and was an addendum to the Historic Scotland architect's report for the building repair grant application. The report included some background information about the original commission, a brief description of the paintings and their execution and a fairly detailed account of Phoebe Anna Traquair's technique based upon documentary sources and laboratory analysis of paint and varnish samples which were carried out specifically to inform decisions about the conservation of the murals. Although access was limited this third inspection provided an opportunity to judge the rate of deterioration of the paintings since 1995. Further cleaning trials were carried out and a broad estimate of the work needed and a timescale were provided.

At the same time as Historic Scotland was amassing information regarding the conservation of the murals the City Council part-funded a feasibility study commissioned by Mansfield Traquair Trust which identified possible uses for the building and gave the Trust an indication of the likely costs of repair and conversion. At this time, the Scottish Council for Voluntary Organisations became a partner in the project as future tenant should the Trust be successful in acquiring the building.

The Scottish Council for Voluntary Organisations (SCVO) is the umbrella organisation for the voluntary sector in Scotland and plays a vital role in the life of the Scottish community. SCVO needed new premises in Edinburgh with full disabled access, modern information technology, and in-house conference and training

facilities. Mansfield Traquair Trust needed a tenant to give the building a secure future. Each need provided the solution to the other and an ideal partnership was created. In 1996, the newly founded Heritage Lottery Fund awarded the Trust a major grant to save the building.

With Mansfield Traquair Trust established as a credible potential developer with an end-use, end-user and the bulk of the funding in place, the City Council in 1997 served a repairs notice on the then owners followed by a compulsory purchase order. When the compulsory purchase order was contested, the City Council authorised an emergency repairs notice. This pressure from the local authority encouraged the owners to sell and the Trust purchased the building through an intermediary in February 1998.

### 3.3 A New Use for the Building

The key to the rescue of the Mansfield Traquair Centre was the creation of substantial office space in the under-building to give the building a viable use not requiring ongoing public subsidy. Two floors of offices were fitted into the space beneath the nave (Fig 39) with ancillary accommodation below the chancel and in the attached clergy house. This considerable enabling development was contained within the envelope of the building yet kept the main architectural spaces and the view of the murals unencumbered. The only alteration in the upper floor was a new floor laid on top of the original floor which preserved the original floor and provided under-floor heating and cabling needed for a flexible multi-function space.

*39.   Offices created beneath nave, SG*

The new use would only work if new circulation could be created within the building. Even the widest original stair does not allow two people to pass. The answer was to create a new stair sunk through the floor of the circular baptistery, this required the removal of the original baptistery foundations and the creation of new, deeper foundations (Fig 40).

The comprehensive building repair and alterations contract started in October 2000 with practical completion in August 2002. The Design Team for the building project was led by Simpson & Brown Architects and included Peter Stephen & Partners, Structural Engineers. The main contractor was Morrison Construction Ltd. The building contract included:

- Repair Work included stone repairs using Blaxter stone from Northumberland; repointing as required in lime mortar matching original; missing stone details such as finials recreated; all roofs reslated, new terracotta cresting to roofs to match original; all leadwork and rain water goods renewed, lightning protection installed; new railings to match original; decorative tiling repaired.

- Alterations included the internal ground level lowered by up to 2m to create height for an open-plan office below the nave with mezzanine gallery. Both levels linked to main entrance by foyers below narthex and new stair sunk through baptistery floor (Fig 41). Secondary escape stair, staff accommodation and catering kitchen built in clergy house. Meeting rooms, toilets and service accommodation created below chancel. New oak floor placed on top of original floor in nave. New windows and door to lower foyer below narthex; cills of windows to office area lowered.

- Services renewed: new lighting throughout including specially designed chandeliers for lighting the upper floor and murals; cabling for theatre-style lighting provided to clerestory and lifting points in roof for lighting rigs; all new plumbing; new electrical wiring; ducting for computer and telecommunications cabling.

- Landscaping: holly trees against walls and self-seeded sycamores removed; sitting-out area to north sown with grass and meadow flowers; paths in stone, roadway in tarmac with stone kerbs; rest planted with ground cover ivy with spring bulbs, early summer clematis and late summer honeysuckle.

40.  *Excavation of baptistery foundations, SG*

41.  *Baptistery stair, SG*

### 3.4 Environmental Monitoring

In order to better understand the effect of the condition of the building on the paintings, and to provide information which would inform the design of a heating system, Historic Scotland Conservation Centre (HSCC) installed three 'Smart' readers in March 1999 to monitor relative humidity and temperature levels within the building. After eighteen months the monitoring was continued by Apex Property Care on behalf of Mansfield Traquair Trust with an array of relative humidity and temperature recorders (including an exterior sensor for reference) augmented by moisture sensors fitted by David Hyde Consultants into the masonry at locations of potential risk of moisture ingress: the wall-heads and below valley gutters. In addition, three infra-red thermographic imaging surveys were carried out by Construction Materials Consultants in 2002, 2003 and 2005. Copies of the reports by HSCC, Apex Property Care, David Hyde Consultants and Construction Materials Consultants are held by HSCC and Mansfield Traquair Trust.

It was important not only to have a record of conditions in the building before refurbishment work, but also to gain information about the differences that the refurbishment and the heating system made to environmental conditions.

The data collected show that although the environmental conditions within the building before the heating was installed were cold and damp, the walls had been drying out since the emergency repairs carried out by the City of Edinburgh Council in 1993 and that the internal surface layers appeared to be sufficiently dry to permit full restoration of the paint and plaster. This was borne out by the condition of the paint and plaster found during trials.

Once the building was in use, the basement office space was heated, which had an effect on the church above, quite apart from the new under-floor heating in the church and the wall radiators. The effect of the heating was recorded and monitored. The data was used to inform the heating regime in the building to ensure that the surface of the murals was not warmed too fast, endangering the paint and plaster layers. While average relative humidity dropped quite dramatically after the heating was installed, it was noted that conditions inside the building continued to be influenced by external conditions; in other words, the walls, although fairly thick, provide surprisingly little thermal buffering (Fig 42). This will always have been the case and it seems that the paintings have survived the general ambient conditions very well. It was the severe building failures that caused most problems.

The relative humidity and temperature monitoring was discontinued at the end of the restoration of the murals when it was apparent that the building had adjusted to the presence of heating. Monitoring of masonry moisture levels were continued as part of the maintenance procedures established for the building.

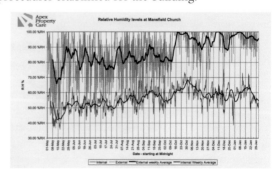

42.  *Temperature and relative humidity record, Mansfield Traquair Trust*

## 3.5 Work on Murals during Building Contract

During the building works the murals in the nave were protected by being covered with a breathable membrane (Fig 43) and those in the chapel and north aisle boxed in. Although a window of breathable membrane was fitted to the partition, it was found that the relative humidity in the north aisle was rising. A dehumidifier was installed for six months in the winter of 2000-01 when the danger of condensation was greatest. When the protection was removed, the only area showing any further deterioration was the top of the Cain and Abel mural of the Adam and Eve panel (Fig 44). This area was protected with more Eltoline tissue.

43.   Protective membrane over nave murals, SG

44.   Detail of Cain and Abel mural showing crackle, salt efflorescence, paint loss and crumbling plaster, HS

### 3.5.1 North Aisle Ceiling

In November 2001 damage was caused to the painted ceiling by repair work to the roof above. Rot had been discovered in the timbers abutting the east wall of the nave and reinforcing metal plates were set in with resin from above (Fig 45). While the reinforcing work was underway, a section of decorated lath and plaster (about 25cm square) was dislodged. Fortunately it survived the fall largely intact. The fragment was removed to HSCC for safe-keeping.

45.   Reinforcing plates strnegthening rot-affected joists of north aisle, HS

The roof, made of timber rafters with lath and plaster infill, had been designed in such a way that there is very little space indeed between the painted ceiling and the sarking boards of the roof above. This meant that in several instances the nails used to lay back the sarking boards pierced through the painted plaster of the bays (Fig 46). In addition to this specific damage the hammering of the roof repair work caused some cracks to form in the lath and plaster work and thin bands of paint loss developed along the join between the timber rafters and the plaster infills (Fig 47).

46.   Nail damage from roof repair, HS

47.   Damage from vibration from roof repair, HS

A protective facing of Eltoline tissue was applied with gelatine solution to all areas weakened or damaged by the impact of the nails. Any pieces of fallen plaster whose location was known were set back in position using lime mortar and faced with tissue. Any vulnerable plaster edges were pointed with lime mortar. Strips of facing paper were applied along all the joins between the timber rafters and the plaster infills (Fig 48).

48.  Facing of weakened areas and relocation of dislodged plaster, HS

### 3.5.2 Nave Spandrel Panels

Scaffolding had been erected in the nave of the church during building works. The painted decoration in the spandrel panels (largely lost) had been inaccessible during previous inspections. Advantage was taken of the scaffolding to look closely at the few surviving fragments, report on their condition and apply any necessary emergency protection in an attempt to ensure their preservation until the conservation of the murals was underway. In the second bay from the east about six or seven plaster fragments of various sizes survived. For the most part they were concentrated along the top of the wall, although three extended down towards the top of the window (Fig 49). The majority of the fragments had extremely little surviving paintwork, however, there was sufficient paint on some to decipher the design.

49.  Hanging fragment in spandrel, SG

Some emergency treatment was considered necessary in order to hold everything in place. The surface was carefully dusted to remove salts and dust and facing of two layers of Eltoline tissue and one of silk crepeline was applied to the surface with a gelatine solution. Wherever possible the plaster edges were pointed with a sand/lime mix (Fig 50).

50.  Spandrel fragment with edges pointed, HS

### 3.6 Photographic and Graphic Records of the Murals

There are no drawings or sketches of the paintings apart from two sketches of pairs of figures for the west wall, dated 1900, in Carlisle Museum & Art Gallery which may postdate the murals rather than be studies or proposed designs (see Fig 73). Traquair often reworked images from her own body of work to use them within a completely different type of painting or artefact. A working design close but not identical to that of the border of the south wall of the chapel is with McGill University collections, Montreal, Canada. No other drawings or sketches are known.

Some early photographs of the murals survive (Fig 51 and see Figs 5 & 27).

The first systematic series of photographs were taken in 1982 by the Royal Commission on the Ancient and Historical Monuments of Scotland (RCAHMS). This record covered the north and south walls of the nave in detail and general views of the west wall and chancel arch. The photographs are in both black and white and colour and copies are held both by the RCAHMS and Historic Scotland Conservation Centre. The 1982 RCAHMS survey did not include the chapel or north aisle. The RCAHMS carried out a second photographic survey in 2000 after the building had been purchased by Mansfield Traquair Trust.

Photographs were taken during the HSCC inspections and the RCAHMS and HSCC photographs together provide a comprehensive survey of the paintings by Traquair and information about the rate of deterioration of the paintings. Those of 1982 are particularly interesting because at that date the paintings were in a good state of repair, although very dirty. The rapid decline of the building during the late 1980s meant that most of the serious losses date from after this survey. The 1982 RCAHMS survey therefore provided a valuable resource for the conservation project.

51.    *1945 view of church showing loss of spandrel panels, RCAHMS*

52.   *Scaffolding of chancel arch and chancel ceiling, SG*

# 4  CONSERVATION – PRELIMINARIES

## 4.1 Planning the Conservation of the Murals

Finding a team of conservators to undertake this project was always going to be problematic. However, the combination of having a large project to be completed, and the perceived need in Scotland for conservators able to take on such a task, gave rise to the idea of using the project to provide a training opportunity for young conservators.

Through the Conservation Bureau, Historic Scotland runs a series of conservation internships each year that allow young or newly trained conservators the opportunity of gaining work experience. The Bureau scheme was extended to encompass an innovative partnership between Mansfield Traquair Trust and Historic Scotland whereby a significant training element was incorporated into the restoration of the murals.

Two members of the Historic Scotland conservation staff were seconded to the project to manage a training programme. This consisted of internships for three young conservators finishing their training and shorter work placements for students of relevant UK training courses and other Historic Scotland training programmes. Private-sector and overseas conservators were also involved. Having one team undertake the conservation work ensured continuity and consistency. The Historic Scotland staff were on site throughout the project and were responsible for all issues relating to Health and Safety, scaffolding (Fig 52), planning and implementing the conservation work. Throughout the project the church was used as a venue for events, and this had to be taken into account whilst planning the work.

Conservation took two years starting in September 2003. For both practical reasons and to suit the requirement of grant-giving bodies the work was divided into two phases. The first phase October 2003 – February 2004, was a trial period during which the various methods and materials needed in the conservation of the murals were tested and which provided the information upon which to more accurately predict the timescale (and thus the cost) of the main project. The chapel was chosen for the trial phase because it is a miniature of the church, a discrete area which could be isolated, and the paintings on its walls and ceilings presented many of the technical problems expected to be encountered elsewhere in the building.

The second phase, February 2004 - October 2005, was the conservation project proper. The programme was dictated by timing and duration of elements of major scaffolding. The work progressed as follows;

| February 2004 | Fragments in Spandrel Panels |
| March 2004 – Sept 2005 | The Nave Panels (work interrupted for work on west wall and chancel arch and chancel ceiling) |
| June – August 2004 | The West Wall |
| Jan 2005 – March 2005 | The Chancel Arch and Chancel Ceiling |
| April and September 2005 | Baldacchino |
| July – Oct 2005 | The North Aisle |

The restoration was recorded: photographs were taken before restoration, at key moments during the work and afterwards; diagrams of the condition and treatment were generated (see Appendices); materials and methods were recorded; and all summarised as two restoration reports (one for each phase). These reports, augmented with photographic and video recording of both building and mural restoration undertaken by Mansfield Traquair Trust, provide a complete record of the whole project and will be invaluable not only as a record but in case any work on the murals should be required in the future.

## 4.2 Philosophy of Repair

Many of the decisions regarding methods and materials were made during the conservation process. Decisions were based on the success of a given material and its ease of use.

One of the main aims was to use the least toxic materials that would work for any procedure, even if this sometimes took a little longer. There were several reasons for this, relating principally to Health and Safety issues. For the conservators themselves, when working for such a long period over such a large area it was both undesirable and uncomfortable to work with toxic materials that necessitated the use of cumbersome personal protective equipment. The building was used for functions in the evening and at weekends, therefore the general public would be affected by any materials used. Furthermore, the disposal of the waste produced presented an environmental hazard.

Another aim was to use traditional materials as much as possible. Such materials have their drawbacks, but these are well known and documented. Reversibility was clearly desirable; however, it is important to recognise that reversibility is closely connected to the nature of the substrate; even the most easily reversible materials are difficult to remove from a very porous substance. It was therefore important not to introduce any material that was completely alien to the original, and whose future behaviour was unpredictable. For the interns and students it was important to become aware of the original materials of the paintings, since this would increase their understanding of different methods and materials generally, and inform their work on the murals. Every effort was made to fully understand Phoebe Anna Traquair's technique, and, where appropriate (such as with the relief work) to repair like with like. Using the Historic Scotland workshops, the conservators each reproduced the artist's method on timber boards, including making up the preparation layers and the pigment media. This proved invaluable in understanding the nature of the paintings.

The owners of the building, Mansfield Traquair Trust, hoped that the paintings could be restored as well as conserved. Thus, missing areas were to be re-created, particularly where there was earlier photographic evidence. The aim was to display the interior as close to its original appearance as possible. Missing sections of gilded relief work were to be replaced and re-gilded where necessary. Areas of lost paint were to be recreated, and the surface was to be given the same satin sheen that it would have had originally.

In the case of missing sections for which there was no, or very little information about the appearance from photographic records, such as the decoration in the spandrel panels which was lost within thirty years of the paintings' completion, it was considered neither possible nor desirable to recreate the missing design. In areas where substantial amounts of paint were missing, for example the central bay of the south wall of the nave (the Joseph panel), but where the losses had occurred since the decoration was recorded by the RCAHMS in 1982, it was considered desirable to reconstruct the missing sections and complete the original image using the photographs for information. All reconstructed sections have been painted in a way that is recognisably different from the original using completely reversible paints.

The wide crack across the Noah panel on the south wall presented particular problems. The crack had formed and been repaired well before the photographic survey of 1982. The band of lost design had been recreated by the previous restorer at some time in the first half of the 20th century. Whilst cleaning the painting during the conservation work it became clear that this reconstruction was not very accurate, either in colour or design. Several original lines at either side of the loss had

been ignored resulting in a slight misinterpretation of the design. With the agreement of the Trust the decision was reached to reconstruct the missing band, even though there was no photographic evidence for precisely what had been there originally. The surviving lines on either side of the crack provided sufficient information to guess quite accurately how the painting must have appeared. The method used to recreate the missing section was a combination of Traquair's technique and the pointillist method used elsewhere to in-paint losses.

## 4.3 Study of the Artist's Technique and Laboratory Analysis

In order to reach decisions about the nature of the decay of the paintings, and the best methods of repair, it was important to have fairly precise information about the original technique.

Contemporary accounts documenting Traquair's technique proved extremely useful but these needed to be verified and a considerable amount of analysis, both visual and laboratory, was undertaken. The bulk of this was done for the production of the 1999 report and the results of this analysis were used to inform the conservation when the project began in 2003. Further analysis was done during treatment whenever it was considered necessary.

### 4.3.1 Contemporary sources regarding the artist's technique

Traquair's technique aroused some interest among her contemporaries and a certain amount was written about her method at the time but nothing by the artist herself.

She was working at a time when technique was considered an extremely important element in art, and when technical experiments were being made. Mural painting was one of the painting methods that experienced a considerable revival of interest during the 19th century. This gave rise to efforts at devising a technique for painting on walls which could survive the British climate but retained the freshness of true fresco. Pioneers in these experiments were Thomas Gambier-Parry and Frederic, Lord Leighton who developed and used the spirit fresco method.

The spirit fresco medium consisted of a complicated (and perhaps slightly explosive!) mixture of beeswax, elemi resin (a soft oil-dissolving vegetable resin), copal varnish (made from a hard, waterproof fossil resin), oil of turpentine and spike oil (distilled from spike lavender), cooked to a workable consistency. The pigments were ground up in this medium and put into tubes. The wall surface and the ground layer were saturated with the medium diluted with turpentine to ensure that when the paint was applied it would bond well with the underlying surface (as it does in true fresco). And Gambier-Parry particularly specified that the plaster surface be rough to enhance penetration of the medium.

Lord Leighton's technique was close to Gambier-Parry's but he found painting on the rough surface difficult. He preferred a smoother ground which he achieved by using finer sand and applying more ground coats, in two of which he included zinc white.

Neither of the above methods was entirely satisfactory either from the technical point of view or in their resemblance to true fresco.

Traquair drew on both these experiments and evolved her own far simpler and in many ways more effective method. This was recognised by Frank Morley-Fletcher (Bibl 9), first Principal of Edinburgh College of Art, in his lecture to the Edinburgh Architectural Association in 1909 during which he praised her technique and relayed *'notes given me by Mrs Traquair of her method of work and preparation of the walls'*. In his lecture notes the method is listed as follows:

1.  A good plaster ground was prepared then successive coats of zinc-white were given, thinned very much at first with oil and turpentine. Almost no zinc in first coats - four or five coats given in all.

2.  The painting was done on the solid zinc-white ground, the colour being ordinary oil colour in tubes, thinned by a medium of beeswax dissolved in turpentine - about one teacupful of beeswax shavings to a pint of turpentine. The lights were got by wiping with a rag, no white paint being used.

3.  The finished painting was varnished with a good copal carriage varnish.

4.  A wash of wax and turpentine is put over all the varnished surface and rubbed by hand with a cloth to a dull eggshell polish.

The freshness and effect of the technique depended upon the partial exposure of the white ground to provide highlights.

The research during the investigative phase in the chapel found that this description of her technique seemed to be broadly correct, although there were slight variations in the ingredients of the ground layer (see below). It is interesting to note that Morley-Fletcher did not refer to the surface having any roughness or texturing. It is possible that his notes are more associated with the painting of the Song School which is onto a smooth plaster surface.

The rough plaster surface advocated by Gambier-Parry when developing his spirit fresco method, was specified to improve the penetration of the medium. Traquair's interests may have been different, and relate more to the visual effect. The roughness adds a vibrancy to the colours and increases the reflective qualities of the paint.

### 4.3.2 Observations based on visual and laboratory analysis

**Substrates** – The paintings are onto four types of substrate; stone, plaster, timber and lath-and-plaster. The walls are made of masonry blocks covered in plaster except for dressed masonry edging and architectural elements. Most of the paintings on the walls is onto a plaster surface, but there are places where the paint goes directly over the masonry (for example the stone moulding of the chapel ceiling) (Fig 53). The paintings on the ceiling of the chapel are onto timber boards. Those in the north aisle are painted onto the timber joists of the ceiling, with a lath and plaster infill between the joists.

53.   *Painted timber string course and stone moulding, HS*

*Plaster.* On the walls there are two plaster layers. Cross section analysis carried out in 1999 shows the layers clearly: a rough lime-based white plaster first coat made of lime mixed with coarse sharp sand, with a smoother pinkish plaster skim coat over (lime mixed with sand and tinted with iron oxides) (Fig 54). The rough surface of the lower plaster shows through and the float marks are clearly visible (Fig 55). The roughness of the plaster varies a little from wall to wall, with the north and south walls of the nave being uniformly rough, while the decorative band on the west wall is slightly smoother. The plaster of the chancel arch and west wall is generally smoother than that of the nave walls.

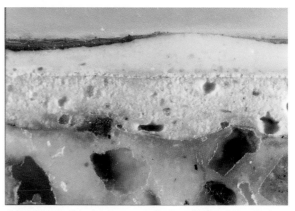

54.   *Cross-section showing coarse plaster, pink skim coat and white priming (magnification x 25), HS*

55.   *Visible plaster float marks, HS*

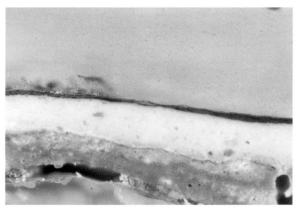

56.   *Cross-section showing salts causing the bond between coarse plaster and skim coat to fail (magnification x 25), HS.*

It is difficult to be certain quite how the layers were applied. It seems that the roughness is principally in the lower, coarser layer, where the aggregate was drawn to the surface with the float. The upper layer may have been rubbed on so that the coarse aggregate would protrude through – grains of sand may be seen on the surface of the plaster immediately beneath the paint. The way in which the layers have separated at the join between the pink skim coat and the rougher base coat due to later damp problems indicates that the bond between these two layers is a weak point (Fig 56).

*Timber.* The boards of the chapel ceiling are set E-W and at each end of the ceiling is a moulded timber framework. The ceiling rises from a string course made

57.   *Close and open joints between ceiling boards, HS*

of a bevelled timber moulding resting on a projecting stone moulding. All of the timber elements described have been painted, as has the stone moulding. (see Fig 53 above). The design is reminiscent of Scottish medieval or renaissance building such as the Guthrie Aisle, now in the National Museum of Scotland, the Skelmorlie Aisle at Largs or the church at Grandtully which have painted decoration.

Originally the ceiling planks would have been very tightly jointed (tongue and groove), and the preparatory ground for the painting would have concealed the joints so that the surface appeared unbroken. However, the wood has since shrunk, so joints have widened, and the scenes are now slightly disrupted by the joint lines (Fig 57).

*Lath and Plaster.* The north aisle ceiling was made to appear more like the Scottish board and beam ceiling which developed into a widespread tradition during the 17th century. Although here the bays between the beams are not made of timber boards but are of lath and plaster. The beams or joists are of softwood.

**Ground layers or priming –** Over the plaster are white priming layers. According to Morley-Fletcher's account (Bibl 9) successive coats of zinc white were applied as a priming. The analysis of 1999 showed several white ground layers. The layers are yellower and more translucent near the plaster suggesting that the first coats were richer in medium (Fig 58). This conforms with Frank Morley-Fletcher's account of the layers having been applied more thinly at first. However, these ground layers are not of zinc white as recorded by Morley-Fletcher, but consist of lead white extended with barium sulphate, chalk and probably silica. Zinc is only detected on the west wall of the chapel in the relief areas and may have been an incidental inclusion in the composition mix.

The wall surface is characteristically rough. On all walls except that of the chancel arch, this is achieved by plastering in a coarse mix. On the chancel arch, especially the lower panels, the roughness is achieved by

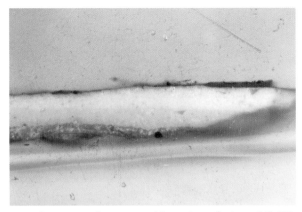

*58.   Cross-section showing ground layers (magnification x 25), HS*

*59.   Textured surface of ground layer of chapel ceiling showing thicker varnish in grooves, HS*

*60.   Detail showing scratching of surface, HS*

applying the later layers of the priming very thickly using a wide brush. This method was also used on the boards of the timber ceiling of the chapel (Fig 59) although the mouldings have been left smooth. The plaster surface of the bays in the north aisle ceiling have a similar sandy roughness to that found in parts of the nave walls, but the surface of the timber joists has been left smooth.

**Paint layer –** One of the artist's aims was to create her images in pure, glowing colours. She achieved this by painting in a fairly transparent paint film over the white ground. The paint is documented as being oil colours mixed with a paste made of beeswax and turpentine. And it is striking how frequently the colours are pure unmixed pigments, applied thinly and often spread with a rag, or fingers, and scratched with a sharp tool (Fig 60).

Seen both with the naked eye and under the microscope (Fig 63), it is possible to see that the paint film contains very little pigment. Under the microscope the pigments appear as thinly scattered particles in a viscous medium. This is also how the paint film looked when observed from close up. Pigment analysis confirmed that a fairly restricted palette had been used: terre verte, viridian, ultramarine blue, iron oxide earth pigments; ochres, umbers, siennas, carbon black. Pink coloured lakes were observed, and red and yellow lakes were also tentatively identified (pigments analysed by polarising light microscopy and SEM-EDX analysis).

*61.   White paint on cherubim of chancel arch, HS*

The results of medium analysis by gas chromatography and mass spectroscopy (carried out by Dr Singer, University of Northumbria, Newcastle-upon Tyne) have been somewhat inconclusive, making definite statements about the composition of the paint and varnish difficult. Most samples gave positive results for linseed oil, however, beeswax and resin components are harder to detect. There was some (if inconclusive) evidence for the presence of beeswax, but no evidence for resins.

During cleaning in the chancel of the chapel (see below) it was found that the lettering of the text at the base of the ceiling had been painted over the first varnish. The reason for this was not obvious – possibly to make the letters stand out more strongly and appear almost in relief. This application of outlines over the varnish was also found in the main part of the chapel. It is found extremely rarely on other parts of the decoration.

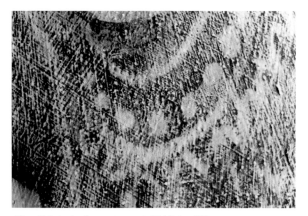

62.   *Paint wiped away to create highlights, HS*

63.   *Cross-section showing paint and varnish layers (magnification 25), HS*

On the chancel arch Traquair used quite a lot of white paint (Fig. 61). But elsewhere she achieved highlights by wiping away the colour to allow the white ground to show through (Fig 62), and white paint was used sparingly.

From the thickness and density of the paint on the upper walls of the chancel arch it seems that here the ratio of oil paint to wax paste was much higher than on other parts of the decoration. This may be because parts of this section of the decoration were painted by John Fraser Matthew.

**Varnish –** Traquair is said by Morley-Fletcher (Bibl 9) to have applied a 'carriage varnish' – probably a copal

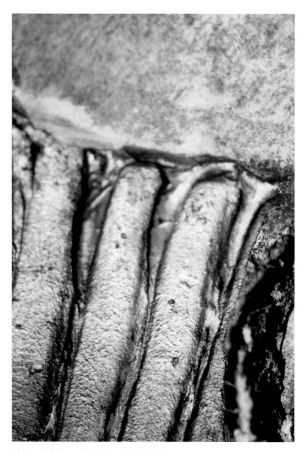

64.   *Gilding with bole visible, HS*

varnish. When this was dry she spread a wax paste, made by dissolving beeswax in turpentine, over the paintings, which she polished up to a satin shine. It is not clear if any of these original finishes survive.

Under magnification, most samples show at least one varnish layer and more usually two (Fig 63). The top (later) layer is generally thinner and darker than the lower (earlier) varnish, which is thicker, clearer and yellower. However, laboratory analyses have not provided conclusive information about the varnish types, or whether the varnish contains any beeswax (see below). The upper layer of varnish is more soluble in acetone/methylated spirits which indicates that it is of the dammar/elemi/mastic type (all being tree resins: dammar a natural tree resin which remains soluble and soft, elemi a soft oil-soluble vegetable resin and mastic a natural tree resin which becomes hard and brittle with age). The lower layer is much less soluble, but cannot be properly identified.

The triterpenoid resins (e.g. mastic, gum elemi and dammar) are difficult to detect with gas chromatography and mass spectroscopy and so it is possible that they are present. The diterpenoids (e.g. sandarac, copals, copaiba balsam) should be detected by this method and so their absence implies that she did not use an oil-soluble resin within the medium or indeed for the final varnishing. From which one must conclude either that the account by Morley-Fletcher indicating that she used a carriage varnish (or copal) is incorrect, or that this layer has been removed during previous cleaning and revarnishing. A very insoluble yellow varnish was found at the top of the west wall and on the west wall of the north aisle (see Appendices 2 and 7) and it is possible that this was all that remained of an original copal varnish.

The oil on the relief areas was a non drying oil, but, until more conclusive evidence becomes available the assumption is that the medium was a traditional linseed oil with some beeswax added. The presence of varnish in the medium is uncertain but it is likely that the paintings were given a protective varnish coat.

65. *Relief of oil lamp in chapel, SG*

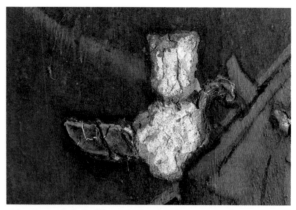

66. *Lost relief of oil lamp in chapel, SG*

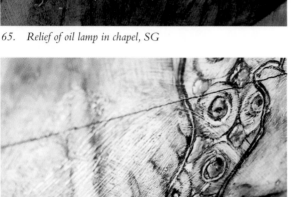

67. *Nail providing key for paste, HS*

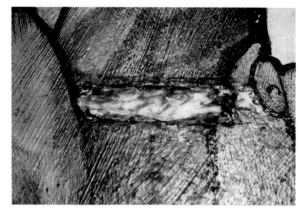

68. *Damaged gilder's putty showing cotton wool, HS*

**Metal leaf** – Metal leaf has been used widely to great effect. Evidence for a type of bole (red preparatory layer) is visible in places (Fig 64). Both gold and aluminium leaf were used, and both were often quite thickly varnished.

**Relief work** – Some decorative elements were built up in relief (a technique also found at the Song School). These include haloes, decorative borders, the oil lamps of the virgins, etc (Fig 65). The relief work was applied over the plaster and ground coats and where it had fallen off it was possible to see a key incised into the lower plaster layer (Fig 66).

The artist appears to have experimented with a range of different materials to make the relief. The greatest variety was found in the chapel where it had been made in three different ways. In the chancel of the chapel it was made of a very hard grey material, probably containing some rosin. Where the paste was missing from the timber surface one could see that here the artist had used nails to provide a key (Fig 67).

On the west wall of the chapel the relief work was made of a composition mix ('compo'), containing whiting, animal glue, linseed oil and rosin. On the south wall it was made of gilder's putty, a mixture of whiting, animal glue and a little linseed oil, with what looks like string or cotton wool to give it added bulk and form.

On the walls of the north aisle Traquair returned to the composition mix. However, in both the chapel and north aisle it is the composition mix that has become brittle and shrunk. Perhaps the artist became aware that this mixture was not so successful, because elsewhere in the church she used the softer gilder's putty exclusively, bulked out with cotton wool and string where necessary (Fig 68).

Metal leaf (mainly gold) had been applied to all areas of relief work.

69.  *Squaring-up mark, HS*

70.  *Change in position of hands of Christ, HS*

## 4.4 Phoebe Anna Traquair's Technique

### 4.4.1 Preparation and transfer of the design

When working on such a large scale an artist would almost inevitably have had to produce preparatory sketches. These would have been useful both to inform the Catholic Apostolic congregation of the artist's proposed decoration, and also for the artist herself in the planning and arrangement of the compositions.

However, as has been noted above, very few of these survive. Furthermore we have very little information about the way the artist transferred her compositions on to the walls. The only wall where there is clear evidence of transfer is the west wall where squaring up marks and other indications of a geometric laying out are visible (Fig 69). This may be the only wall where she used this method, because it is the only part of the decoration where the scale demanded it. Even on this wall the positions of several figures and details have been altered as work progressed. The outlines of the Christ figure, for instance, have been changed, as have the position of his hands (Fig 70).

On the chapel ceiling the artist seems to have plotted out the broad geometry of the design free-hand, probably using her sketches as models. Numerous changes have been made on this part of the painting, as if much was being worked out as the painting progressed. This is borne out by the discovery of a tiny sketch on the ceiling. The paint is so transparent that it is possible to see a quickly executed sketch which shows the artist working out how to arrange two of the figures (Fig 71). The sketch was then painted over with the final composition.

In several instances the artist is clearly working independently of a 'plan', such as on the ceiling joists of the north aisle, where she has sketched designs, but in the event painted something rather different (Fig 72).

The possibility that one of the few surviving sketches – that of an angel and mortal embracing on the west wall – may not be a preparatory sketch, but an image based on the painting, reduces further the number of sketches that we have to help understand how the artist worked (Figs 73 & 74). But it is likely that many of the heads and figures of the decoration were fully worked out beforehand and, if not transferred directly, were used as models for the design.

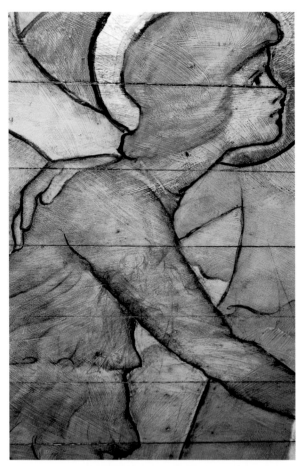

71. *Sketch of a pair of figures on the chapel ceiling, painted over by the upper arm of the figure in the purple robe HS*

72. *Sketch design different from painted design, HS*

73. *Sketch of angel embracing mortal, Carlisle Museum and Art Gallery, RCAHMS*

74. *The painting as executed, SG*

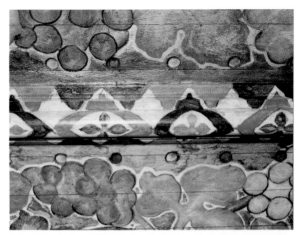

75. *Detail of moulding in chapel showing speed of execution, HS*

76. *White over-painting on lilies in chapel, HS*

77. *Strong black outlines, HS*

The overall impression is of an artist who, while undoubtedly planning and preparing her designs and compositions to quite a high degree of detail, nonetheless had both the tendency and ability to make important changes when actually executing the painting. Indeed the number of places where one may see alterations is so great that to cite each example would involve a lengthy list. The more significant changes have been noted in the Appendices.

### 4.4.2 Execution

The speed at which Traquair worked may be seen very clearly on the timber mouldings of the ceiling of the chapel. Here the paint has been put on quickly, with little concern for neatness of finish, since the overall effect is all that would be seen from the ground (Fig 75). Some of the energy of the decoration must be attributed to this way of painting, and it would appear that the artist wanted to retain this sense of freshness and vivacity.

There are several instances where the artist reworked her painting. The most obvious cases are where she has blocked over areas in white paint. This may be seen clearly on the lilies on the south side of the ceiling (Fig 76). In other places reds have been strengthened and sometimes ochre shading has been applied over the main colours. Some of these changes seem to have been made after varnishing and are therefore very soluble.

A very characteristic design feature is the strong black outlines around figures and elements. Most of these outlines appear to have been applied after the first varnishing. The outlines range from being a single line,

78. *Feathered edges, HS*

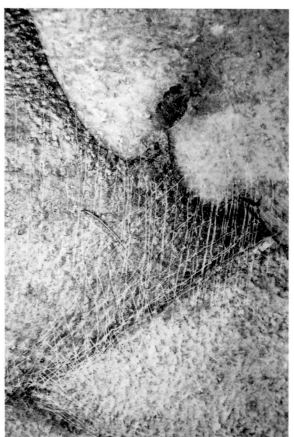

79.  *Painting style of Doubting Thomas medallion, HS*

80.  *Thin colours wiped over surface, outlines scratched, HS*

for instance around haloes, to being a smudged feathered edge as seen around the decorative borders in the chapel (Figs 77 & 78).

The technique of her 1924 recreation of the Doubting Thomas medallion, where she repainted an area approximately 1m square on the lower part of the east end of the south wall of the chapel (see diagrams in Appendix 1 and Fig 31), is similar to her original method, but the repair plaster is much smoother and the painting style far more detailed, with small brushstrokes much closer in style to her miniature work and not the thin paint and wiping out of her earlier paintings (Fig 79).

### 4.4.3 Success of Phoebe Anna Traquair's Technique

By the time Phoebe Anna Traquair embarked upon this series of wall paintings the technique that she had developed proved itself to be very efficient and successful.

One might expect a combination of oil paint on plaster to be less enduring. Normally plaster and oil paint do not bond well together. The paint layer forms a distinct film which tends to separate from the plaster surface. This problem seems to have been avoided by having the thick priming layer as a buffer between the oil paint and the alkaline plaster. Also, the method of rubbing oil and turpentine into the dry plaster before applying the lead white priming layers and ensuring that the first

coats of the priming were very thin, containing a large amount of turpentine (a method adapted from the spirit fresco technique) has meant that these two surfaces are well bonded. By having the later priming coats thick, Traquair achieved the desired roughness and a good solid unabsorbant surface on which to apply the oil based paints.

Where the building had not been affected by damp the paintings were in very good condition. This indicates that the method evolved by the artist did not present inherent failures.

Using a slow-drying wax paste medium over a non-porous priming layer afforded the artist plenty of working time. The colours could be wiped back, blended, and etched before they had completely dried, and changes could be made without much difficulty. By the same token the method allowed the artist to work extremely quickly, which is a characteristic of her style. She could cover large areas, blocking in the colour by brush and spreading it out at quite a speed using a rag, brush or, more often than not, fingers or the palm of her hand. The method was also ideally suited to her aim of achieving a glowing and translucent effect. The lightness of the ground shines through the thin paint film, making it appear bright and glowing. The use of pure pigments heightens this effect, as does the use of placing complementary colours beside each other.

As noted above, she often broke the outlines by scratching through them with a small tool, or the wooden end of her brush which added both softness and liveliness (Fig 80).

Another very lively technical adaptation by Traquair is found in the relief work. The final method that the artist settled upon was particularly simple and effective. Warm gilder's putty was applied both as it was, or bulked up with cotton wool, depending on the amount of relief required. The mixture dried quickly and several layers could be applied in quick succession. It was also lightweight, meaning that a considerable thickness could be achieved without becoming too heavy. In Traquair's hands this technique was used in an original and dramatic way. The bands of flowing gold emanating from Christ's Aura on the west wall are a powerful and exciting piece of design (Fig 81).

Traquair's confidence in her technique developed as she progressed, and she also appears to have painted increasingly quickly.

From the conservator's point of view, the simplicity of the technique is striking. On the whole, the paintings were not built up in numerous complicated layers. The paint may seem thin because it contains very little pigment, but the waxy oil medium provides a thickness and strength. The simplicity of the technique is effective both visually and technically, and makes working on the paintings more straightforward and a real delight.

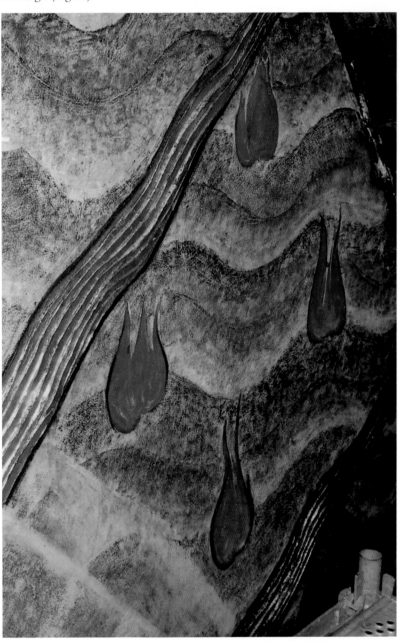

*81.   Example of raised relief work, HS*

# 5 CONSERVATION

## 5.1 Condition of the paintings before conservation

A general account of the conservation procedures is given here. The Appendices to this report contain a detailed description of the condition of the murals before conservation and a full record of the methods and materials used in the conservation of each part of the painting. Methods are plotted on diagrams used to record the condition and conservation processes.

Generally, it is true to say that where the condition of the building fabric was good; the paintings had survived in excellent condition. The varnish layers had become extremely dark and dirty, but the paint and plaster were relatively sound.

It is likely that environmental conditions alone might not have had an adverse effect on the paintings, and it was the failures in the building fabric that really caused a serious deterioration in their condition. The damp that had penetrated the building due to poor maintenance

82.  *Detached paint, HS*

caused much damage to both the paint and plaster. Large sections of plaster, particularly beneath the string course on the south wall of the chapel and in the central bay on the south wall of the nave had become detached. Thanks to the emergency facing tissue applied during the 1990s by Historic Scotland staff, there were only a few areas of plaster loss – apart from the spandrel panels where the plaster had fallen off decades before – but by then there had been paint losses.

Wherever the plaster was weak, but also in several places where the plaster had remained secure, the paint had become detached (Fig 82). Virtually every part of the decoration had some weak paint, but in the better preserved areas this was restricted to isolated patches. For instance the paint was often weak over the red line painted around the panels in the nave (Fig 83). However, where the paint had been affected by salts the paint was inevitably seriously damaged. Thus large sections of the Joseph panel, the Entombment scene, the Betrayal scene, the Cain and Abel scene, the lower part of the south side of the chancel arch and numerous areas in the chapel were very badly affected.

Gilded relief work was in variable condition, depending largely on how it had been made. The best preserved type was the gilder's putty mix, the mixture containing resin had become very brittle and had shrunk away from the wall surface. This latter mixture was found exclusively in the chapel and the north aisle. Fortunately most of the relief work survived in excellent condition.

83.  *Flaking paint over red line of earlier decorative scheme, HS*

Apart from the rot in the north aisle ceiling, wooden ceilings were in good condition. There was some detaching paint on the chapel ceiling and the chancel ceiling, but this was restricted to areas where damp had penetrated from failing gutters or missing slates.

Large settlement cracks had developed in the west, east and north walls, but these had caused relatively little damage to the surrounding paint and plaster.

### 5.2 Trials

During the first, trial, phase of work in the chapel, the aim had been to test as many conservation methods as possible that might be needed. It was hoped that the methods that proved most effective could be used throughout the restoration.

In the event the methods and materials had to be adjusted for the different parts of the decoration. This was partly because the artist herself varied her techniques slightly over the eight or so years that she was working on the decoration. But it was also because some parts of the decoration had been restored in the past, and some areas had been affected differently by damp and salts, and thus responded differently to treatment. Therefore, cleaning and fixing trials were routinely needed before proceeding in the different areas.

For the 1999 report some cleaning trials had been made in order to understand the nature of the painting and also to provide information about the limits and requirements of the cleaning method eventually adopted. These trials provided a basis for subsequent tests. The trials were as follows:

1   Saliva – This removed surface dirt very efficiently, far more effectively than water alone, which indicated that the slightly raised pH of saliva rendered it more active (Fig 84).

2   White Spirit – A small amount of oily dirt was removed with white spirit, but it had no effect on the darkened and dirty upper varnish layer. If there was wax in the later varnish one would expect the white spirit to have a slight solubilising effect.

3   Benzyl Alcohol – This had some effect on the upper varnish but it worked very slowly and unevenly.

4   Isopropanol – A little more effective than 3, but again a very slow and uneven cleaning activity.

5   Methanol: White Spirit mixture – Some effect on the varnish layer but leaving a patchy appearance.

6   Acetone: White Spirit mixture – As for 5, but possibly more effective. Neither 5 nor 6 affected the lower varnish layer.

*84.   Cleaning trials, HS*

7 Methanol (Industrial Methylated Spirits or IMS) - Slightly less aggressive than acetone. The surface took on a slightly smeary appearance whilst cleaning as if the varnish was not being completely solubilised. The varnish nearest the paint layer remained intact but under magnification it was possible to see that the lower varnish surface was slightly affected.

8 Acetone - this removed the later varnish but seemed to be too aggressive and broke through the varnish nearest to the paint although it did leave islands of a very yellow varnish on the surface.

In the event a combination cleaning method was developed (see below), whereby surface dirt was first removed with soap liniment (a slightly methylated aqueous mixture containing volatile oils – eucalyptus, camphor and oleic acid), after which the varnish could be successfully cleaned with industrial methylated spirits. In places where the paintings had been damaged, combinations of IMS, white spirit and acetone were needed, sometimes applied on poultices.

Salt analyses of the plaster from the damaged areas (made with Merck indicator strips) show the presence of sulphates (approximately 400mg/lt), a very slight nitrate content (10mg/lt) and no nitrites. Sulphates were not detected in sound plaster samples and had probably migrated through from the stonework. These results were borne out by chemical analysis carried out for Apex Property Care by Remedial Technical Services of Bourton, Dorset in 2001. The latter analysis also showed no free moisture which confirmed the readings of the moisture sensors.

Consolidation trials - Although PVA had been used in the past it was thought preferable to use an alternative paint fixative because research had shown PVA had a tendency to cross-link and break down. Paraloid B72 would need to be applied in too concentrated a solution which would make removing excess from the surface difficult given the sensitivity of the paint film. The trials with Lascaux Heat Seal 375 were successful due to the adhesive's strong holding properties and solubility in white spirit. The paint film was not affected by heat sealing the adhesive. Water-based adhesives such as gelatine and the acrylic adhesive Primal AC33 were successful on occasions, but sometimes unable to penetrate behind areas where the surface was very badly damaged and crazed due to salt efflorescence. However, Primal AC33 proved an excellent adhesive in places where the salt damage had caused only isolated cracking and tenting.

Lime grouts were successful at consolidating detached plaster, and trials with Ledan TB1 (a proprietary lime grout produced in Germany by Kremer) proved effective, particularly where the plaster was only slightly detached.

Following trials, various methods and materials were chosen with which to carry out the conservation, although, as noted above, variations had to be made on the different parts of the painting.

## 5.3 Conservation Methods and Materials

Generally, the methods and materials were as follows:

### 5.3.1 Initial Dust Removal

The paintings and surrounding architectural features were so dusty and cobwebby (Fig 85) that it was necessary to vacuum sound surfaces before beginning conservation work.

### 5.3.2 Securing Plaster

Where the plaster was loose (the south wall of the chapel; the Joseph panel; the Adam and Eve panel; The Noah panel; the chancel arch) the method was as follows:

1. Make injection holes through the plaster using a needle and small wooden tool – avoiding painted areas as much as possible.

2. Vacuum out any loose disintegrated plaster from behind.

3. Inject a thin lime-based solution: a runny grout made of lime and marble dust. Some Primal AC33 (acrylic adhesive) was occasionally added to this mix when used on the Joseph panel; Ledan TB1 was used on all other panels (Fig. 86).

85. *Dust and cobwebs in chapel, also showing example of wooden plugs in ceiling, HS*

86. *Injecting Ledan TB1 to secure loose plaster, HS*

87.  *Presses holding plaster in place while consolidant sets, HS*

88.  *Injecting Primal AC33, HS*

89.  *Injecting Lascaux Heat Seal 375, HS*

90.  *Heat-sealing the adhesive, HS*

4.  Thicker lime mortar was then fed in behind the plaster to fill the void where necessary, such as on the Joseph panel.

5.  The loose plaster was pressed back for 24 hours to ensure a good bond (Fig. 87).

The above treatment was done through facing tissue. Most of which had been applied (using gelatine) during previous inspections.

### 5.3.3 Securing Paint

Three different methods were used to secure loose paint, depending upon the precise nature of the damage.

**Gelatine.** Flaking paint on wooden substrates was secured using a gelatine solution. Gelatine was also used to consolidate flaking paint on plaster where it was possible to ensure a good spread of the adhesive and the plaster was not too porous.

First the affected area was 'faced up' with paper applied with the adhesive. A more concentrated solution was then injected behind the flaking paint. When the adhesive had cooled, and had started to become tacky, the area was heated and pressed back with a heated spatula. Sometimes it was left overnight before heat sealing. The facing tissue was then removed with warm water.

It was often necessary to make repeated applications and where there was 'blind' detachment, this method was less effective.

**Primal AC33.** This adhesive was very effective at securing large and distinct paint flakes as well as 'blind' detachment, because of its excellent ability to travel behind the loose paint and penetrate small cavities.

The affected area was first wetted with industrial methylated spirits (IMS). The adhesive was injected directly behind loose paint, or dropped through tiny cracks, and tapped into position (Fig 88). After a short time, when the adhesive had started to become tacky, the surface was pressed back with a barely damp cotton wool swab. If the paint was brittle it was also heat sealed, but often this was not necessary.

**Lascaux Heat Seal 375.** This adhesive was used where the surface had been badly affected by salts and which had caused the paint to display a fine crackle and blind detachment over a large area. Usually these areas had already been faced up with paper applied with gelatine. Where there had been further paint loss, new paper was applied directly with the Lascaux Heat Seal.

A 50% solution of the adhesive was applied hot by brush through the tissue. A stronger mix (about 80%) was then injected behind loose paint (Fig 89). This was left for 24 hours to allow the solvent to evaporate, following which the area was heat sealed with a heated spatula (Fig 90). The facings were removed using white spirit, although paper that had been applied with gelatine needed to be removed with a combination of hot water and white spirit used separately. It was often necessary to make

91. *Removing facings, HS*

92. *Brittle relief work in north aisle which had become detached, HS*

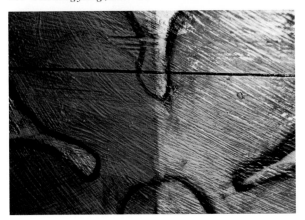

93. *Surface cleaning the painting, HS*

repeated applications of adhesive, and to use the heated spatula as the facing tissue was being removed (Fig 91).

### 5.3.4 Repairs to the Relief Work and Cleaning of Gilding

Depending upon the way it was made, the condition of the relief work varied considerably. When made from the composition mix it had become very brittle and had shrunk and curled away from the wall surface (Fig. 92). It was not possible to lay back the brittle pieces of the most severely deformed sections. Here cavities behind the partially detached fragments were filled with gilder's putty, irrespective of how they had been made originally. Where sections had become completely detached they were set back into a thin film of the putty. Gilder's putty was also used to replace missing sections, the putty being bulked out with cotton wool as necessary.

The metal leaf was generally cleaned with tri-ammonium citrate, thoroughly rinsed with water.

### 5.3.5 Cleaning the Painted Surface and Varnish Removal

As noted above, the method used to clean the paintings had to be varied slightly from one part of the decoration to another. Surface dirt, including bird lime, was removed with warm water and soap liniment applied on swabs. Oily dirt was removed by wiping over with white spirit. Where the cleaning was straight forward, the dirty varnish layer could be swabbed clean with IMS. More stubborn areas could only be cleaned with mixtures of IMS (Fig 93), acetone and white spirit, in varying proportions – often applied in poultices.

Solvent cleaning was done in stages, with the first clean only going so far. It was found that if the paintings were then left for about 24 hours, the second cleaning was easier and more even.

A thin layer of the previous – possibly original – varnish has been left. This means that the paintings are not as bright as they would have been originally, since this layer leaves a slightly yellow film over the surface. Cleaning areas that had needed paint and plaster fixing was very difficult and slow, not least because the surface was weaker and more uneven than elsewhere. Traquair's method of painting onto a rough surface also affected the ease with which the paintings could be cleaned (see Fig 59).

### 5.3.6 Filling losses

Paint losses were filled both to provide a clear surface on which to in-paint, and to build up the surface where the paint was missing so that it was flush with the surrounding paint layer. The filling mixture was made of marble powder and lime putty (3:1), referred to elsewhere in the report as 'fine filler'. Cracks, including the very deep crack on the west wall, were deep filled with a 3:1 lime mortar, followed by the fine filler. Surface cracks were filled with the finer lime and marble powder mix (Fig 94).

### 5.3.7 In-Painting

The fillings were first painted with water colours. Generally, if the loss was small, the paint was built up to match the surrounding area before varnishing. In the case of larger losses, and losses within areas where the surrounding paint had been badly degraded by salts, the water colours were used to build up the colour to a limited point (Fig 95). The surface was then varnished and in-painting was completed over this varnish layer using pigments mixed in varnish. The paint was applied in dots so that it is easily distinguishable from the original.

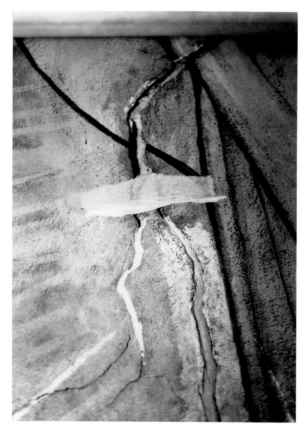

94. *Filler and fine filler in deep settlement crack on west wall, HS*

95. *Water colour in-painting in small dots over filling, HS*

As noted above the large filling on the Noah panel was treated slightly differently – see also Appendix 4.

### 5.3.8 Varnishing

The paintings have been given two types of varnish. First a pure dammar varnish – which is fairly glossy, but wets out the colours. Second a matt dammar varnish which leaves a satin finish close to the original polished wax paste that the artist used. The matt varnish is made of 50cc bleached beeswax pellets in 50cc pure gum turpentine and 400cc of dammar varnish. The second type of varnish was applied warm.

For the most part two coats of each varnish were applied. Only on the better preserved nave panels was one layer of each type sufficient. The final varnish layer was spread on using a cloth to ensure an even distribution (Fig 96).

The first varnish coat was applied after cleaning and before filling. Subsequent varnish layers were applied during the in-painting process. No varnish in-painting was done onto an unvarnished surface. The varnish therefore performs the dual function of being a varnish coat and an intermediary layer between the original paint and any in-painting.

### 5.3.9 Chancel Ceiling

This was perhaps part of the same basic decoration of red lines on the nave panels that preceded the Traquair scheme. The white oil ground for the stencil design had been painted over an earlier varnish, followed by the oil colours and gilding of the stencil. The decorative bands of textured paper were tacked to the timber ceiling. The whole surface had then been given a protective size coating.

The general condition of the chancel ceiling was good. But some remedial work to lay back isolated flaking paint was required, and the surface needed cleaning. The size coat had crazed and shrunk noticeably, and in places was pulling off the thin paint layer beneath. The size had absorbed dirt and dust over time, some of which had also sunk into the oil paint layer. The paint had peeled away from the surface in isolated places, and the applied paper decoration was also slightly deformed (see Appendix 8).

Loose paint and paper were secured using gelatine. The surface was swab cleaned with a 5% solution of sodium carbonate in warm water to remove the dirty size coating (Fig 97). The ceiling was then given a protective coating of matted dammar varnish. It was decided to varnish this surface after cleaning rather than re-apply a size coat because the varnish would offer better protection from dirt, would not shrink and would be easier to remove in future.

Some minor retouching was done in varnish colours where parts of the stencil design were missing.

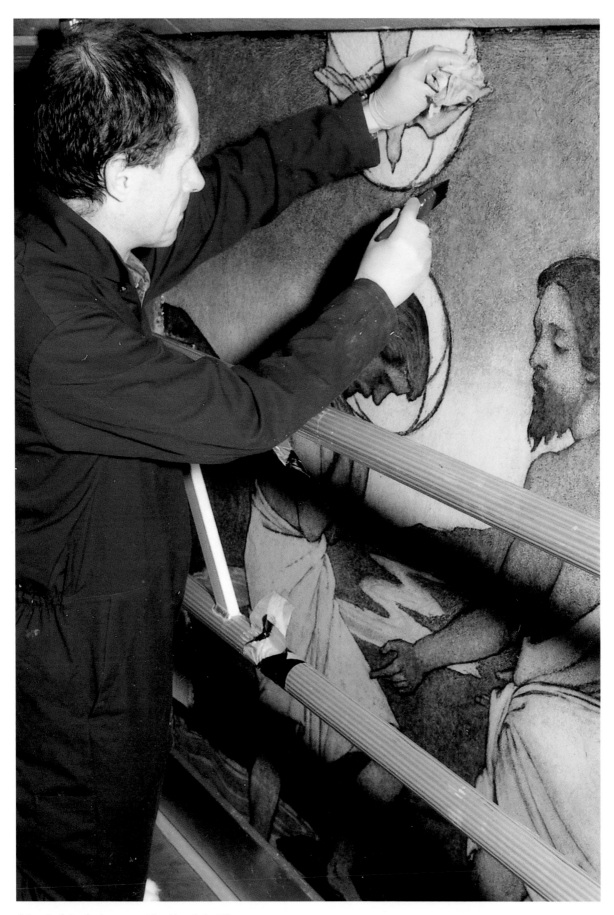

96. *Applying final matt varnish with a cloth, HS*

### 5.4 Maintenance of the Conserved Murals

#### 5.4.1 Building

The building is now maintained by the tenant (the Scottish Council for Voluntary Organisations). A maintenance programme has been agreed with regular inspections of rainwater goods and other areas which, if there were problems, could endanger the integrity of the fabric of the building and survival of the murals. In addition, a quinquennial inspection by an architect appointed by Mansfield Traquair Trust will ensure the building is properly maintained.

#### 5.4.2 Temperature and Relative Humidity

Procedures for the proper control of heating in the church have been implemented. Background heating is provided by under-floor heating with the main radiators only being used to boost the temperature for events. The number of people attending events keep the relative humidity within desired tolerances; a drop in relative humidity occurs only during events attended by low numbers. Shelves have been fitted above the radiators in the nave to deflect rising warm air from the face of the murals; the effectiveness confirmed by the temperature and relative humidity sensors which were positioned in front of the mural panels.

#### 5.4.3 Light

The windows do not have any UV filtering on them, and sunlight strikes the paintings directly – particularly those on the north wall in winter. It would be advisable to try to reduce the amount of sunlight hitting the paintings not only because of the light damage, but also because it causes localised heating of the surface. Perhaps sun curtains would be the easiest option.

#### 5.4.4 Regular Inspections

As part of the maintenance schedule, the paintings will be inspected on a regular basis, so that any problems may be identified early.

97.  *Cleaning chancel ceiling, HS*

# 6 OBSERVATIONS ON THE ARTIST'S STYLE AND TECHNIQUE MADE DURING CONSERVATION

The conservation of the paintings provided an opportunity to look at them at close quarters. This can allow one to assess an artist's work slightly differently. Although many parts of this decoration were designed to be seen from a distance, the closer view can give some insights.

## 6.1 General Observations

As noted above, the subject matter of the decoration was decided by the leading members of the Catholic Apostolic congregation. However, it seems that the interpretation of the commission and the stylistic means of expressing the various biblical references were left to the artist.

At first glance the murals read as a whole, and they were clearly conceived as such. However, the decoration is divided up into discrete parts, each with its own particular theme, mood and role within the scheme. Although the technique used by the artist remained fundamentally the same throughout the years that she was decorating the church, changes in style and approach are noticeable. It is difficult to be certain to what extent these are due to the natural progression of the artist's style over time, or were pre-planned variations made to correspond with the different moods or functions of the various elements of the decoration. For instance the narrative style of the paintings in the chapel and north aisle is not quite the same as that used for the scenes in the nave.

*98.   First panel of Wise and Foolish Virgins parable, west wall of chapel, SG*

High on the chancel arch, figures are painted in a bold manner using a limited palette (red, black and gold), which are easily read from a distance (see Fig 273 in Appendix 3). The scenes in the chapel and north aisle were to be seen from closer up, and are painted in a dense flowing style. The figures have the curving dance-like stance and clinging garments reminiscent of Italian renaissance and pre-Raphaelite paintings (Fig 98). In the chapel and north side aisle Traquair makes extensive use of relief work. Haloes and frames around scenes are modelled and gilded and large parts of the patterned decoration is highlighted with metal leaf. The plaster surface is generally slightly less rough than the surface in the nave, and the effect is richly coloured and jewel-like.

The highly decorative floral friezes and the densely patterned north wall of the north aisle pay homage to Traquair's association with the Arts and Crafts tradition established by William Morris (Fig 99).

The panels of the north and south walls of the nave are spare and simple by contrast (Fig 100). These scenes are reminiscent of the contemplative paintings by the French mural painter Puvis de Chavannes (1824 -98) (Fig 101).

In these scenes Traquair rarely uses metal leaf or relief. Relief work is only found in the Annunciation scene and in the David and Solomon panel, which are at diagonally opposite ends of the nave walls (Fig 102). Elsewhere gilding is limited to fine gilded lines such as on Christ's halo on the north wall (Fig 103).

The surface of the plaster in the nave is generally quite rough, and the paint has been applied thinly, which adds to the stunning simplicity and clarity of these scenes.

The relatively quiet and even tempo of the nave panels is reinforced by the way each panel has been divided equally into three separate scenes. Several scenes have great dramatic strength, such as Christ in the Wilderness, the Betrayal, Cain and Abel, but there is nonetheless a simplicity and stillness about them which is in part due to the serene sky and landscape settings (see Fig 100). The scenes represent biblical stories that form the basis or foundation of the Christian faith.

*99. Dense floral pattern of north aisle, SG*

*100. North wall of nave, Christ in the Wilderness panel, SG*

*101. Painting by Puvis de Chavannes*

*102. King David, raised work of coronet and harp, SG*

*103. Calling of the Disciples, gilding limited to fine lines, HS*

The two large end walls (the chancel arch and the west wall) create a strong and 'noisy' contrast to these quiet but intense narrative scenes. These may be said to illustrate the visionary and, more particularly, the Catholic Apostolic interpretation of the message of the bible stories depicted on the walls.

The chancel arch, painted at the start of this enormous commission, is the part of the decoration over which the artist seems to have spent the most time, and possibly encountered the greatest difficulties. It is clear, particularly in the lower scenes, that she made several changes to the composition, and that she reworked quite a lot of the detail.

For instance, she had originally painted a decorative border around the panels containing the Cherubim (Fig 104). This was approximately 15cm wide, and contained a fairly elaborate scroll design. The framing border would have had the effect of firmly enclosing the figures within the architectural framework, and meant that they would have been a little smaller. Removing the border results in the rainbow and sky background spanning across the empty space of the open arch.

The composition is thus brought right up to the surface. A border might have created a sense of depth and would have given the viewer the impression of looking into a defined space. Disposing of the border also has the effect of uniting both sides of the arch within a single composition.

These changes have not been made at the plotting out stage (as is frequently the case elsewhere), but after the painting had already been wrought to quite a high finish. One can clearly see that the positions of the figures have had to be altered (Fig 105), and this has involved a lot of blocking out over the previous design.

Another significant change on the chancel arch is in the row of twenty-four elders. At first Traquair painted a classical capital on the columns of their canopied seating. However, she changed the form of the seat design so that the columns finish with a simple 'scroll' shape, reminiscent of a more primitive Byzantine design, with resonances of the early eastern church (Fig 106).

*104. Original border of cherubim panel visible through the paint layer, HS*

*105. Detail of change in position of cloak, HS*

*106. Outline of earlier capital visible through the red paint, HS*

The paint is quite thick in places. Extensive use has been made of white paint, and the colours have frequently been built up in several layers and shades (Fig 107).

## 6.2 Comparison of Chancel Arch and West Wall

It is interesting to compare the painting of the chancel arch with that of the west wall – these two great surfaces tackled eight years apart. It is also interesting to wonder to what extent the differences between her handling of these two walls is due to Traquair's evolution as an artist, or was envisaged from the outset as a means of conveying a different mood. Possibly a fortunate mixture of the two.

Clearly the subject matter is totally different. The west wall illustrates the Second Coming. Above the frieze the

*107. Detail of upper part of chancel arch, HS*

entire wall has been left as a single surface broken only by the wheel window. And the composition has been conceived as one enormous event or 'moment in time' – with Christ appearing, surrounded by singing and trumpeting angels (Fig 108).

*108. West wall after conservation, SG*

The wall surface of the chancel arch by contrast is already articulated by a series of string courses and decorative mouldings, and the artist has used this to divide her composition into bands, each one illustrating a part of the biblical text, and the whole being a representation of the church infinite – and therefore 'timeless'.

The west wall is conceived as a very three dimensional vision; an open sky receding between two hillsides, and Christ seeming to float towards the viewer. In the case of the chancel arch the emphasis is on the two dimensional surface. The divided composition and dense surface patterning reinforce the impression of looking at a screen – reminiscent of the rood screen or iconostasis of the early church – an emblem of the division between man and heaven or eternal truth (compare Fig 108 and Fig 3).

In the lower ranges of the west wall angels are painted as if against a landscape, greeting and comforting souls. The naturalistic flowers are all in bloom, symbolising a moment of maturity (Fig 109). There is a lively sense of movement and heightened emotion.

The translucent paint has been applied thinly so that the ground layer glows through as it would a glaze, and predominantly pure, simple colours have been used. Although the artist did make some changes, these are at the sketch stage, and so the overall impression is one of clarity, ease and speed of execution with little evidence of re-working (Fig 110).

In contrast to this the symbols of the evangelists on the lower panels of the chancel arch are set within a dense grid pattern. As if placed over the vertical and horizontal grid is a rich diaper design in gold lines with gold and blue dots (Fig 111). Different colours have been pulled across the surface, making it difficult to see precisely what colours have been used. This mesh of ornament is very two-dimensional, but with its own mysterious sense of depth. It is as if the artist is trying, through means of technique and design, to create the sense of mystery, and timelessness evoked in the texts. In the deep background blue of the cherubim is a deep green swirling design (Fig 112), which momentarily transforms what appears to be sky, into sea.

109. *Accurate representation of flowers in bloom, HS*

*110. West wall, blue paint applied quickly and thinly, HS*

*111. Chancel arch, lion, one of four holy beasts, HS*

*112. Background of cherubim panel, HS*

*113. Trumpeting angels on west wall, SG*

*114. Trumpeting angels on chancel arch, SG*

On the west wall the trumpeting angels are blowing hard into their trumpets, which are held at an angle; and the singing angels display intense emotion on their faces (Fig 113), which is all part of the expression of moment and humanity. The angels on the chancel arch by contrast have impassive and expressionless faces. They are ranged in straight lines and their trumpets are held parallel (Fig 114). This is both a literal depiction of the text, and an evocation of stillness and timelessness. On these two walls Traquair is depicting the foundations and the culmination of the Catholic Apostolic faith.

In addition to the variations caused by the different moods that Traquair wished to create on these two walls, there had also been a development in her style of painting as well as in her technique. This is clearly illustrated by comparing her treatment of the 'sea of glass and fire' at the tops of the end walls. On the earlier chancel arch the sea of glass is painted in a rich painterly style. The paint has been applied thickly and different colours have been spread beside each other without waiting for the paint to dry, so that they blend together on the wall. When looked at closely the brushwork is reminiscent

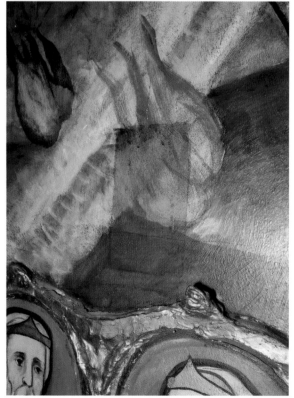

*115. The sea of glass on the chancel arch during cleaning, HS*

*116. The sea of glass on the west wall, HS*

*117. Heads of angels on west wall (during cleaning), SG*

*118. Heads of angels on chancel arch, HS*

of a modern Expressionist painting (Fig 115). On the later west wall the colour has been applied extremely thinly and sparely, with parts of the wall unpainted. The brushstrokes are large, free and closer in style to an Impressionist painting (Fig 116).

It is interesting to see Traquair experimenting with portraiture on the upper parts of the west wall (Fig 117). Although several of the angels on the chancel arch are evidently likenesses, their absence of expression gives them a somewhat studied and idealised anonymity (Fig 118). Many of the angels on the west wall, however, are evidently portraits of the same sitter looking not only in different directions, but frequently portrayed in a different way and style, and with different expressions. They are remarkably lively and free, with great character and immediacy, a striking contrast to the more highly finished and 'perfected' images of angels lower down the wall.

It is possible that her interest in catching a moment or fleeting expression was influenced by developments in photography (see Fig 117). True portraits are also to be found on the chancel arch, however. One of the elders in particular appears to be based on a portrait (Fig 119).

It is possible to identify the hand of John Fraser Matthews, who assisted Traquair on this part of the decoration. Several of the 'multitude of the redeemed' have clearly been painted by him (compare Fig 120 with Fig 121).

*119. One of the four-and-twenty elders (after conservation), HS*

*120. Head by Traquair, HS*

*121. Head by Matthews, HS*

And it would seem that some of the elders were at least finished off by him (Fig 122).

### 6.3 Spandrel Panels

Originally the spandrel panels at the top of the north and south nave walls were painted. From the scant remains and few early photographs one can see that there was a procession of angels set against a modelled and gilded background, possibly with a trellis with flowers in the foreground (Fig 123).

The colours of this fairly narrow band of wall surface were the rich greens, reds and gold of the trumpeting angels of the two end walls (Fig 124). This would have created a visual link uniting the two end walls. It would also have provided a much needed framework for the nave panels beneath, and by so doing would have emphasised the liturgical connection between the end walls as well as the significance of the Bible stories illustrated beneath to the fundamental beliefs of the Catholic Apostolic Church.

The impact of the loss of this part of the decoration has perhaps passed unnoticed because it occurred so long ago. However, without this framing element the nave panels do not seem quite so well integrated into the decorative scheme, and a powerful element of the original conception has undoubtedly been lost.

122. *Elders' heads by Matthews (left) and Traquair (right), HS*

123. *Spandrel panel: trellis design, SG*

124. *Rich colours of spandrel panels, SG*

# 7 CONCLUSION

The outcome of the total project was the rescue of a building with murals of international importance; its restoration and conversion to a viable new use; the restoration of the murals, an increase in the number of trained mural conservators in Scotland; creation of a new events venue and visitor attraction; public access to the murals and their interpretation; and the future maintenance of the building assured.

The project encompassed many aspects which make it exemplary including the involvement of the local and wider community, co-operation between a building preservation trust and a local authority to rescue a listed building, conservation of a Category A-listed building with extensive enabling development contained within the building envelope but which resulted in upgrading of the local environment, local area regeneration and economic benefits. The restoration of murals of international significance was delivered by an innovative partnership with the national heritage agency involving training and work experience for structural painting conservators, interns and students. Enjoyment and appreciation of the murals has been enhanced by improving their presentation and providing physical and intellectual access and by increased knowledge about the artist's technique, the religious significance of the murals and the historic importance of the Catholic Apostolic movement. Above all, this project shows what can be achieved by a group of dedicated individuals starting out with nothing but determination and goodwill.

The conservation of these paintings has been a very rewarding exercise. It has provided an excellent training opportunity for several young conservators. It is salutary in this age of speed that the murals, which Phoebe Anna Traquair created in eight years, have taken over ten man- and woman-years to restore. The cleaning process has restored the brightness of the murals: fawn garments have emerged in pastel shades, muddy greens revealed to be celestial blue, browns have turned to deep, rich reds and dull backgrounds now gleam silver and gold. The beauty of the colours, which are so essential a part of Phoebe Anna Traquair's vision, has been revealed, and parts of the paintings that were in danger of being lost have been set back. And last but not least, the restoration has provided the opportunity to re-assess the work of this undervalued artist.

62

# Key for Condition and Treatment Diagrams

| Condition | | Treatment | |
|---|---|---|---|
| Raised work | | Gelatine treatment | |
| Lost raised work | | Heat Seal 375 treatment | |
| Loose raised work | | Primal AC33/35 treatment | |
| Cracks | | Areas filled and inpainted | |
| Salt damage | | New raised work | |
| New flaking paint | | Areas treated with gilders' putty | |
| Facing tissue 1995 | | Areas treated with lime plaster and Primal AC33/35 | |
| Hollow plaster areas | | Areas treated with lime plaster and Ledan | |
| 1924 Restoration | | | |
| Raised work + aluminium leaf | | | |
| Raisd work + gold leaf | | | |
| Pentimenti | | | |
| Previous repair | | | |

*125. Key for condition and treatment diagrams*

# APPENDIX 1

# CHAPEL – THE PARABLE OF THE WISE & FOOLISH VIRGINS

Parable of the Wise and Foolish Virgins (Matthew 25:1-13): obeying the Divine call and going forth, straying from the way, awakening, filling the lamps. Above arch into nave: Christ and the Traveller. Vignettes providing commentary: (above) Tower of Habakkuk (Habakkuk 2:1-3) *'I shall stand on my watchtower and wait; though the vision tarry, it shall surely come'*, virgin arising, (below) restoration to life of the widow of Nain's son (Luke 7:11-18), Annunciation (Luke 1:26-38), feeding of the five thousand (Mark 6:30-44), Christ with the sleeping disciples (Matthew 26:40), three Marys at the empty tomb (Matthew 28:1), entombment (Matthew 27:57-61), Doubting Thomas (John 20:24-29).

Main ceiling: The Garden of Paradise. Chancel ceiling: Psalm 148: *'Praise the Lord, ye sun and moon, ye mountains and all hills, ye dragons and all deeps, ye fruitful trees and all cedars, ye beasts and all cattle, ye kings and all people'*.

Signatures:

PAT monogram, 1895, west wall, first panel of wise and foolish virgins, lower R H corner

P A Traquair, 1896, west wall, above arch into nave, lower R H corner

PAT monogram, 1896, west wall, above hatch, lower L H corner

PAT monogram, 1896, south wall, above R H window

P A Traquair, 1896, south wall, above L H window

P A Traquair, 1896, chancel arch, lower R H corner

Restored by P A Traquair, 1924, south wall, Doubting Thomas vignette, L H corner

**Raised work + gold leaf**

**Raised work + aluminium leaf**

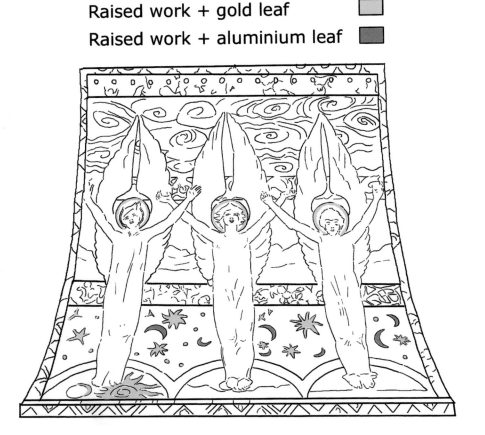

*126. Chapel chancel ceiling, north side, condition diagram*

## Raised work + gold leaf ▢

*127. Chapel chancel ceiling, south side, condition diagram*

### 1.1 Chapel Chancel Ceiling

#### 1.1.1 The Condition before Conservation (Figs 126, 127, 128)

**Support -** The ceiling timbers appeared to be sound. The timbers had shrunk slightly, causing the joints to widen. This affects the appearance of the ceiling, but does not imply any structural weakness (see Fig 57).

The framing pieces are made of fairly short lengths tightly jointed together. The ceiling is divided into two panels by a central timber moulding running E-W along the spine of the vault. A row of circular holes runs on either side of the central moulding. Most of these have been plugged with round wooden pegs (also painted), although some are missing. Some of the pegs have a smooth rounded surface whilst others have been cut off straight (see Fig 85). It is not clear what function these holes perform. However, they are found on all barrel vaulted timber ceilings of the church (nave, chancel ceiling and south aisle) and may have been intended to increase ventilation in the roof space, although this would not explain the wooden plugs that feature both in the south aisle and the chancel ceilings.

**Ground and Paint Layers -** Although very dirty, the chancel ceiling was in good condition. The damp problems noted in the main aisle had not affected the chancel, and the paint and ground were intact, except for some slight mechanical damage caused during the erection of scaffolding. Some small areas of relief work had been lost, but for the most part this was in good condition.

**Relief and gilded elements -** These were made of a very hard material. Where they had survived they were in excellent condition. Where they were missing one could see the nails knocked into the ceiling timber to provide a key (see Fig 67). Both gold and aluminium leaf were used (Fig 129).

#### 1.1.2 Conservation Treatment

**Support -** No treatment required.

**Paint layer -** Very little consolidation was required. None of the paint surface in the chancel had been faced up on previous inspections, and fixing was limited to strengthening paint edges where accidental damage had occurred during the construction of the scaffolding.

64

*128. Chapel chancel ceiling before conservation, RCAHMS*

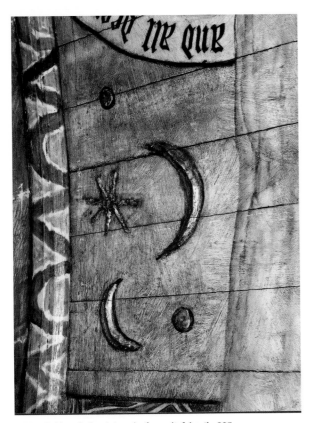

*129. Gold and aluminium leaf on relief details, HS*

Fixing was done with gelatine. A fairly weak solution of gelatine was first applied by brush through Eltoline tissue to hold the weak paint in place. This was followed by injecting a stronger solution behind the weak paint. When the gelatine was nearly dry the adhesive was heat sealed using a heated spatula. The area was left to dry before the tissue was removed with warm water.

Before any cleaning could begin, the entire area was carefully vacuumed to remove cobwebs and dust.

It was found that methanol was the most effective cleaning agent. The best method was to apply the solvent lightly over the surface leaving it quite damp for a few seconds and then wiping the varnish away with a swab that was still quite loaded with methanol (Fig 130).

Where the surface was highly textured the methanol could first be applied by brush, and the dissolved varnish removed with cotton-wool swabs.

Very ingrained dirt – particularly along the string course and on the framing moulding bands at each end of the ceiling – could be removed more successfully by adding an equal part of acetone to the methanol.

*130. Removing varnish from mouldings of chapel chancel ceiling, HS*

When the dirty varnish layer had been removed, it was possible to see a second varnish layer lying immediately over the paint (Fig 131). This layer, although clean, had yellowed slightly. It was slightly soluble in methanol. This may be the original 'copal' varnish applied by the artist – it is unlikely that the wax paste had survived later restorations.

*131. Early varnish immediately over paint, HS*

Although the varnish had yellowed slightly and therefore had dulled the bright intensity of the original colours, it was agreed that it should be left. In addition to being part of the original fabric of the paintings, the varnish also plays a protective role; in places where the varnish had been broken, the thin paint layer with its high wax and turpentine content, was vulnerable and certain colours were fugitive.

The lettering across the lower band of the painting was found to be extremely soluble in methanol. It appears to have been painted over the 'copal' varnish, with the colour possibly mixed in varnish only, or with very little oil content. These areas therefore were not cleaned – the cleaning being taken up to the edge of the letters.

Because the later or upper varnish layer was so dirty the effect of cleaning has been very dramatic (Fig 132).

*132. Chapel chancel ceiling, north side, during cleaning, HS*

**Relief Work –** Cleaned with soap liniment. No repairs were made.

**Varnishing –** The aim was to attain a finish that resembled the final *'wash of wax and turpentine…applied and polished by hand to a dull eggshell finish'* described by Morley-Fletcher (Bibl 9), at the same time as saturating the colours. This was achieved by applying a slightly matt varnish.

The varnish chosen was dammar. Although, in comparison to its synthetic alternatives, this varnish is known to darken over time, it is also known to be completely reversible even after centuries. In addition, its visual properties are yet to be met by a synthetic equivalent. Bleached beeswax pellets were added to the varnish to matt it to an eggshell finish. Following several trials it was agreed that the most successful mixture was made up of 50cc wax pellets: 50cc pure gum turpentine: 400cc dammar varnish. The varnish was applied warm.

Another requirement of any varnish that is to be applied over such a large scale is that it may be applied quite easily either by brush, or by rag. It is not practical to spray a varnish onto a mural of this size. A dammar varnish is far easier to apply evenly by brush than a synthetic varnish such as ketone.

Because the chancel paintings were in good condition and had cleaned very evenly, a single varnish layer was considered sufficient in this part of the church.

## 1.2 Main Aisle Ceiling

### 1.2.1 Condition before Conservation (Figs 133, 134, 135, 136, 137)

**Support –** The timbers were sound, with no signs of rot. The boards seemed to have warped very slightly, and this was noticeable when the ceiling was viewed from the floor of the chapel under certain light conditions.

**Paint and Priming layers –** The paint on the south side of the ceiling was very dirty but both paint and priming layers were in good condition.

On the north side a band of severe and widespread flaking paint was observed at approximately 55-90cm from the spring of the vault (Fig 138). The flaking tended to spread from the edges of the planks where the joints had widened. The widening of the joints had not caused weakness in the paint elsewhere on the ceiling, but in this area the broken edges were distinctly vulnerable. In several instances the paint and priming layer seemed to have sagged to form a ridge that had separated from the timber support (Fig 139). Elsewhere the paint did not appear detached, but, by running the back of one's fingernail over the surface, one could hear that the paint had separated from the timber. The paint flakes were very brittle, and had settled into position as though the damage had occurred quite a long time ago. The position of this band of damage indicated that it was caused by damp penetration due to failing gutters in the valley gutter above. The water would be able to leach through to the surface through the joints between the planks.

**Metal leaf –** In excellent condition.

*133. Chapel main ceiling, SE bay, condition diagram*

*134. Chapel main ceiling, SW bay, condition diagram*

*135. Chapel main ceiling, NE bay, condition diagram*

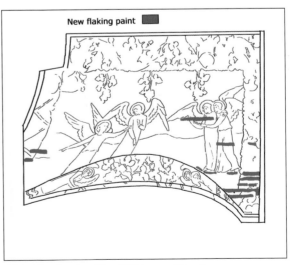

*136. Chapel main ceiling, NW bay, condition diagram*

*137. Chapel main ceiling before conservation, RCAHMS*

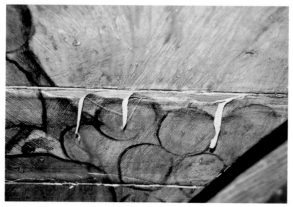

*138. Chapel main ceiling, flaking paint, HS*

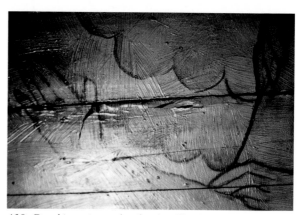

*139. Detaching paint on chapel main ceiling, HS*

### *1.2.2 Conservation Treatment (Figs 140, 141)*

**Support –** No treatment of the support was required.

**Paint and Priming Layers –** Where the paint had become detached, both the paint and priming layers had been affected but the bond between these two layers remained good.

The same method that was successful in the chancel was used in this area, although the damage here was considerably more severe. The method was as follows; the surface was faced up with Eltoline tissue held in place by a weak gelatine solution (Fig 142); a stronger gelatine solution was injected behind weak areas; when the surface was beginning to dry the adhesive was heat sealed using a heated spatula. Where the paint flakes were very large and brittle and were bent at right angles to the timber surface, it was necessary to try and soften the paint first with the heated spatula to encourage it to lie flat. This was partially successful, but in some cases the paint was so brittle that it had to be broken at the point of bending, and then laid flat. The process required several repeat application before the paint was successfully laid back.

**Cleaning –** Once the paint surface was consolidated it could be cleaned by the same method used in the chancel. Whereas the only soluble areas in the chancel had been the black lettering described above, it was found that all of the outlines on the main ceiling had been added after varnishing. It was therefore necessary to clean around all outlines, including the feathered edges of the decorative border. To avoid having the outlines seem too harsh by contrast to the surrounding cleaned surface, a single application of the methanol was made. This reduced the later varnish slightly, but left the outline intact.

As with the chancel, the effect of cleaning was very dramatic (Fig 143).

**Varnishing –** The matt dammar varnish used in the chancel was used on all surfaces. The already quite high gloss of the earlier varnish meant that a single varnish coat was sufficient.

### *1.2.3 Observations*

During work it was noticed that wiring, which travels around the two arches leading through to the chancel, and the light fittings, centred in the arcade, had been painted (Fig 144). This shows that the lighting was installed before the painting of the decoration began. The paint on the wiring had become very brittle and had separated from the plastic coating over the wiring in many places. It was very difficult to re-attach the paint because of the curved surface of the wiring and the failure of the plastic to absorb any suitable adhesives. It was decided to clean this as little as possible (because cleaning weakened the surface) and leave it alone.

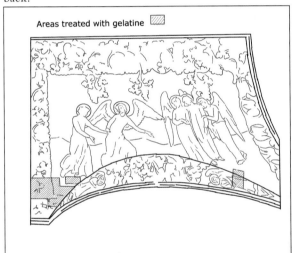

*140. Chapel main ceiling, NE bay, treatment diagram - paint*

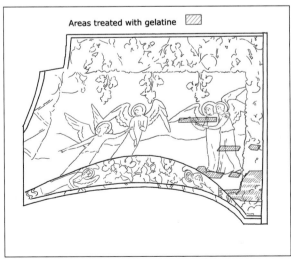

*141. Chapel main ceiling, NW bay, treatment diagram - paint*

*142. Facing tissue applied to areas of flaking paint, HS*

143. Chapel main ceiling during cleaning, HS

144. Painted light fitting and wiring in chapel, HS

## 1.3 Main Aisle Walls

### 1.3.1 West wall – Condition before Conservation (Figs 145, 146, 147, 148, 149, 150)

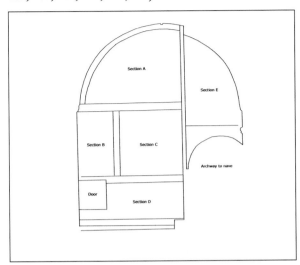

145.  Chapel, west wall, diagram of sections

146.  Chapel, west wall, section A, condition diagram

147.  Chapel, west wall, section B, condition diagram

148.  Chapel, west wall, section C, condition diagram

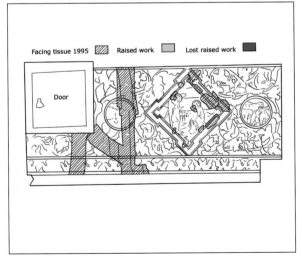

149.  Chapel, west wall, section D, condition diagram

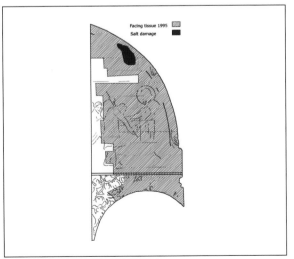

150.  Chapel, west wall, section E, condition diagram

**Support –** The west wall is divided into two sections; a larger area to the south that extends down to approximately 2m from the floor, and a recessed section over the entrance arch. A crack runs down the height of the west wall at a distance of approximately 1.3m from the south corner, and there are some smaller cracks adjacent to this in the lower panel. A protective facing was applied to the crack in 1995. None of these cracks appeared new and the plaster was stable.

The recessed section of the wall over the entrance was badly affected by the damp. This area had been faced up in 1995 (Fig 151). Salts could be seen efflorescing copiously on the adjacent unpainted masonry, and this sort of efflorescence will have occurred beneath the paint layer. A cross section photograph from 1999 illustrates the effects of salts on the adhesion of the plaster layers (see Fig 56).

*151. Chapel, west wall, before conservation, RCAHMS*

**Paint** – The paint on the main part of the wall was in good condition. The paint over the entrance was badly affected by salts, it had been lost in places and was detaching over a wide area. When the facing tissue was removed it was possible to see that this area had been retouched in the past, possibly during the comprehensive cleaning undertaken at some stage between 1923-42 (Fig 152). The surface was also badly stained by runnels, presumably caused by water running down from the roof space above.

**Relief work** – The relief work around the medallions in the frieze had shrunk and cracked quite badly. Small lengths were missing and several pieces were loose (Fig 153). Some repairs had been done during previous inspections and the area had been faced up to ensure that no further losses occurred.

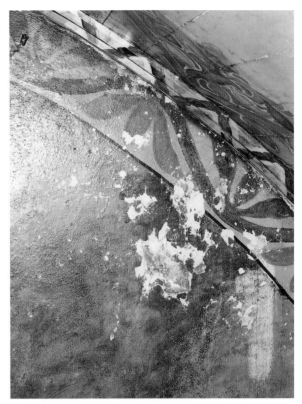

*152. Previous retouching within areas of missing paint, HS*

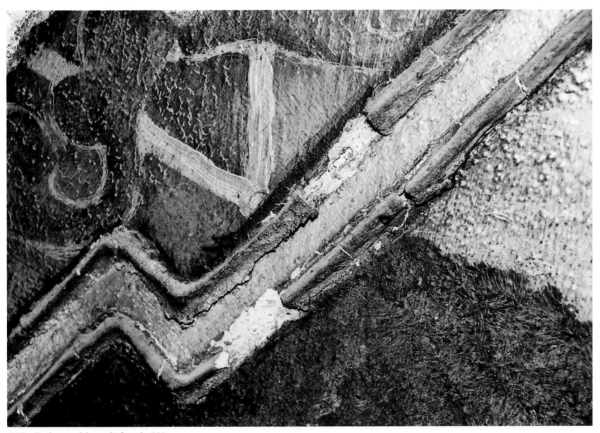

*153. Broken and lost relief work, HS*

### 1.3.2 South wall – Condition before Conservation (Figs 154, 155, 156, 157, 158, 159, 160, 161, 162)

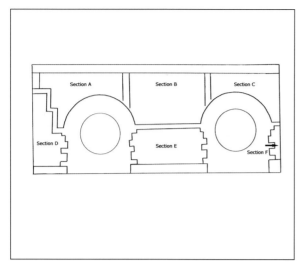

154. *Chapel, south wall diagrams*

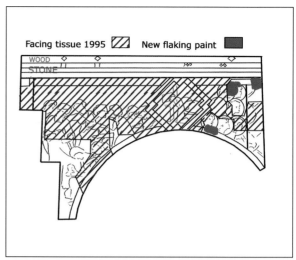

155. *Chapel, south wall, section A, condition diagram - paint*

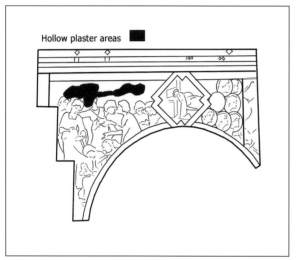

156. *Chapel, south wall, section A, condition diagram - plaster*

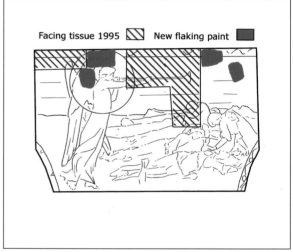

157. *Chapel, south wall, section B, condition diagram*

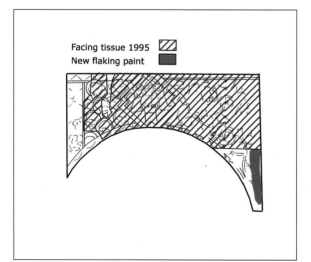

158. *Chapel, south wall, section C, condition diagram*

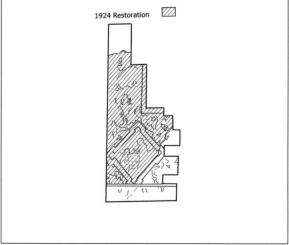

159. *Chapel, south wall, section D, 1924 restoration diagram*

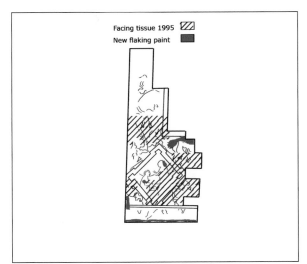

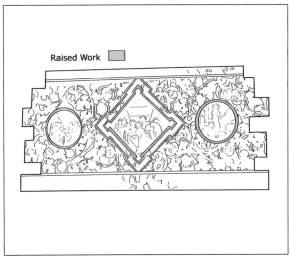

*160. Chapel, south wall, section D, condition diagram*

*161. Chapel, south wall, section E, condition diagram*

**Plaster –** Damp entering along the wall-head had pushed the plaster off the walls along a band approximately 50cm wide. The worst damage was at the east end of the wall. Some plaster had been lost, but the protective facing applied in the 1990s had kept most of it in place (Fig 163).

Further down the wall the plaster was sound. However, there must have been problems in the lower left corner, because it is here that the artist had to return in 1924 to make repairs (see Fig 31).

**Paint –** Where the plaster had been affected by damp the paint was in a very bad way. Before being faced in the 1990s large sections of paint and the priming layer were flaking off (Fig 164). There was also widespread blind detachment. However, the characteristic fragmentation of the paint due to salts efflorescing on the surface, found on the nave panels, was not so noticeable. Most of the upper part of this wall had been faced up in the 1990s.

**Relief work –** It was on the south wall that Traquair first used the soft gilder's putty to make the relief framework to the central medallion. Other than some minor mechanical damage it was in excellent condition.

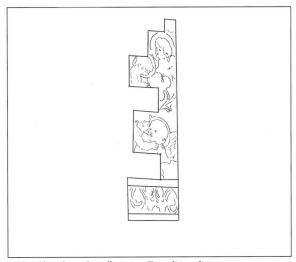

*162. Chapel, south wall, section F, condition diagram*

*163. Band of damaged paint and plaster with protective tissue, HS*

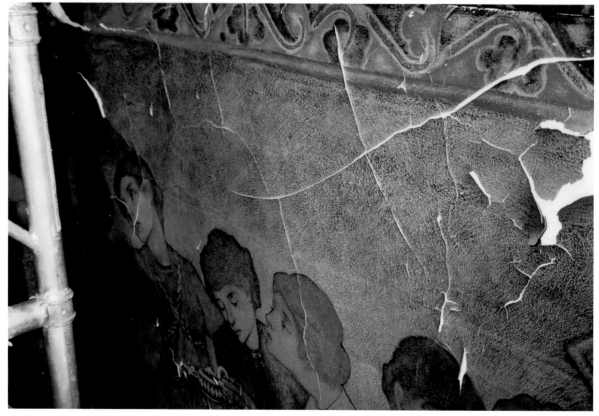

*164. Paint and priming layers flaking off, HS*

### 1.3.3 East wall (chancel arch) – Condition before Conservation (Fig 165)

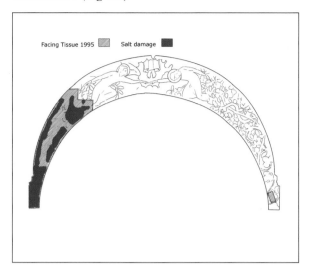

*165. Chapel, east wall chancel arch, condition diagram*

**Support –** Painting on the east wall is limited to the narrow chancel arch above the string course (Fig 166).

Most of the plaster on this wall was intact, with the exception of a fairly large section in the north-east corner, corresponding to the position of the valley gutter. Here the plaster had been broken up by salts and was quite powdery, with the surface missing in places (Fig 167). The stonework had also been broken by salt damage.

**Paint –** This area had been faced up in 1995, but large parts of the facing had since become detached because the surface was so powdery. Paint loss had already occurred previous to the application of the protective facing, and it is difficult to judge whether the condition of the painting had worsened since then. Much of the

paint at the base of the wall where it meets the string course had disappeared completely.

The painted border beneath the lower scenes responded differently to cleaning. It is possible that this had been restored at a later date.

### 1.3.4 North wall – Condition before Conservation

Originally, small sections beneath the string course were painted. However, these are now completely lost due to salt damage. The stone of the string course is also very powdery and broken in places (see Fig 167).

*167. Serious salt damage and paint loss on chancel arch and adjacent stonework, HS*

*166. Chapel, chancel arch, before conservation RCAHMS*

### 1.3.5 West Wall – Conservation Treatment (Figs 168, 169, 170, 171, 172, 173)

168. *Chapel, west wall, section A, treatment diagram*

169. *Chapel, west wall, section B, treatment diagram*

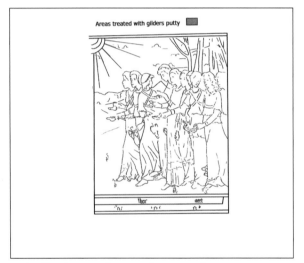

170. *Chapel, west wall, section C, treatment diagram*

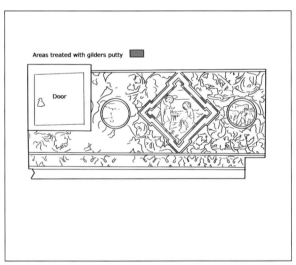

171. *Chapel, west wall, section D, treatment diagram*

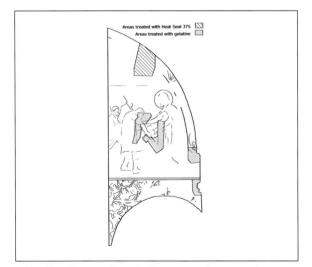

172. *Chapel, west wall, section E, treatment diagram - paint*

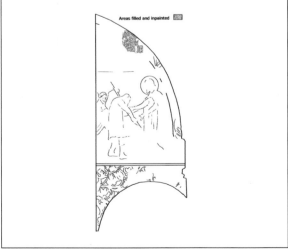

173. *Chapel, west wall, section E, treatment diagram 2*

**Support –** No treatment of the plaster was necessary.

**Paint –** Damp-damaged paint on the recessed surface was consolidated first with gelatine. This was partially successful and allowed the facing tissue to be removed. Further consolidation was done with Lascaux Heat Seal 375.

The damaged area was very difficult to clean. The water runnels over the surface had left a noticeable stain, which previous restorers had tried to conceal with retouching (Fig 174). Poulticing was fairly successful, but it was necessary to glaze over the runnels in order to reduce their appearance (Fig 175).

*174. Retouching over water stains by previous restorers, HS*

175. *Chapel, west wall, after conservation, SG*

## 1.3.6 South Wall – Conservation Treatment (Figs 176, 177, 178, 179, 180, 181)

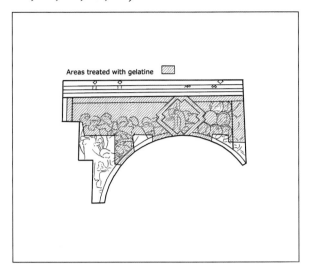

176. *Chapel, south wall, section A, treatment diagram - paint*

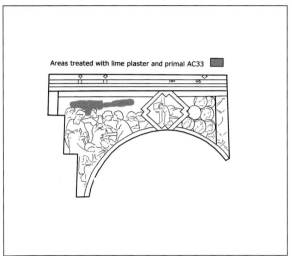

177. *Chapel, south wall, section A, treatment diagram - plaster*

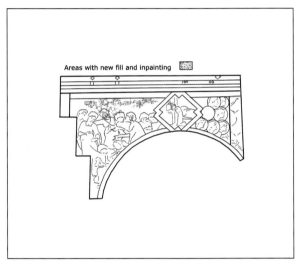

178. *Chapel, south wall, section A, treatment diagram 3*

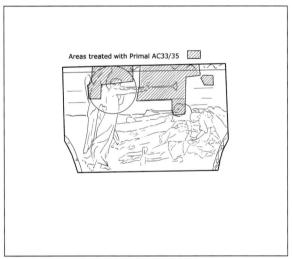

179. *Chapel, south wall, section B, treatment diagram*

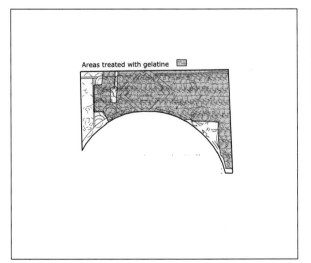

180. *Chapel, south wall, section C, treatment diagram*

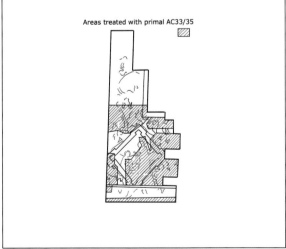

181. *Chapel, south wall, section D, treatment diagram*

*182. Making holes through facing tissue, HS*

*183. Vacuuming out loose plaster, HS*

*184. Injecting lime slurry, HS*

*185. Initial consolidation with gelatine, HS*

**Plaster** – Loose plaster was re-attached using a lime-based slurry followed by a lime grout. Holes were made through the facing tissue (Fig 182) and paint and priming layers and loose plaster was extracted using a vacuum (Fig 183). Fresh lime-based slurry was injected behind (Fig 184). In the first instance this was done with a lime casein mix, however this did not travel well behind the plaster and the method was adapted. A mix of lime slurry and Primal AC33 was first injected, followed by the thicker lime grout. The plaster was held in place with presses until the grout had set (see Fig 87).

**Paint** – On the badly damaged area beneath the string course, consolidation was first done with gelatine in order to be able to remove the facing tissue (Fig 185). Once the tissue had been removed consolidation was completed using Primal AC33. Other isolated areas of detached paint such as in the repaired area in the Doubting Thomas panel were consolidated with gelatine.

Those areas which had been consolidated were difficult to clean with IMS alone. Poultices of IMS and acetone were needed to remove the varnish from stubborn areas (Fig 186). Most of the remainder of the painting could be cleaned with IMS; a band adjacent to the window, however, where water had been running over the surface, was also difficult to clean with swabs, and required poultice cleaning.

Cleaning the section that had been recreated by Phoebe Anna Traquair in 1924 proved slightly problematic (see Fig 31). The variation in the artist's technique meant that the surface responded differently (Fig 187). It did not have the same varnish layers, and the paint layer itself was not the same as the surrounding original work. The paint had been applied in very short brushstrokes, and may not have contained wax paste. It had also been painted in a colour that matched the surrounding mural with its, by then, darkened varnish layers. Tri-ammonium citrate was used to clean the paint surface (Fig 188). The colour difference became very marked once the surrounding early paint was cleaned (Fig 189).

**Relief work** – Conservation was limited to consolidating the damaged edge with gelatine.

*187. Cleaning surface of 1924 recreated mural, HS*

*188. Tri-ammonium citrate used to clean the 1924 recreated mural, HS*

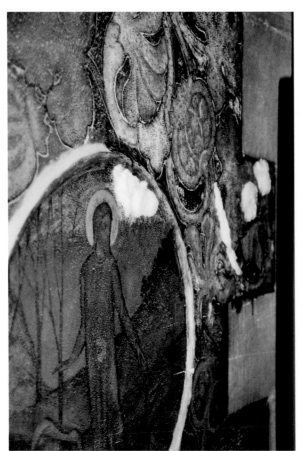

*186. Cleaning difficult areas with poultices, HS*

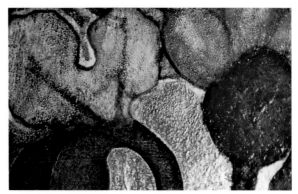

*189. Colour difference between 1896 original and darker 1924 restoration, HS*

### 1.3.7 East wall (Chancel Arch) – Conservation Treatment (Figs 190, 191)

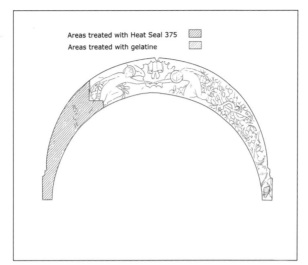

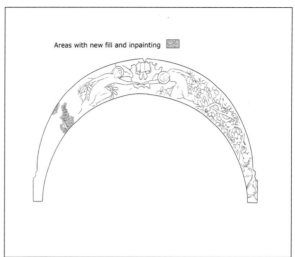

190. *Chapel, chancel arch (east wall), treatment diagram*

191. *Chapel, chancel arch (east wall), treatment diagram 2*

**Paint consolidation** – A true assessment of the condition of the paint was difficult through the several layers of facing tissue. In the first instance consolidation was done with gelatine. The facing tissue was wetted with a weak solution of gelatine so that the damage could be seen more easily. A stronger solution was then injected behind the paint layer. The surface dried more quickly than when consolidating the ceiling, and the paint could be heat sealed within quite a short time (Fig 192).

Once the surface was consolidated sufficiently, the previous facings were removed so that the damage could be seen and assessed more easily. It was found that where several layers of facing tissue had been applied, this operation was more difficult (Fig 193).

Further tissue was then applied to allow a second application of the process wherever necessary.

Where the tissue had separated from the wall, a lot of dust had settled behind it, making consolidation very difficult. Wherever possible the loose tissue was folded back from the wall surface and the dust removed with cotton swabs soaked in cold water. Sometimes the paint was attached to the tissue, but occasionally it had remained attached to the wall, which made removing the dust a bit more difficult.

On the whole, gelatine was a very successful consolidant. However, it was not completely effective where there was a lot of blind detachment and widespread cracking of the paint surface. Here the gelatine failed to penetrate sufficiently through the fine fissures in the surface. Further trials were made using Lascaux Heat Seal 375 and wax resin paste. Both of these methods were successful. The Lascaux Heat Seal is slightly more toxic, but it is easier and quicker to use.

**Cleaning** – Wherever possible this was done after fixing with gelatine and before trials using other adhesives to ensure that the dirty varnish was not consolidated with the paint and therefore more difficult to remove. For the most part cleaning was done with methanol as described above. The runnel marks and staining on the west wall proved to be very stubborn; the addition of 50% acetone allowed these areas to be cleaned more effectively.

Once the damaged area on the east wall had been consolidated adequately, the dirty varnish was removed. The gelatine remaining on the surface had to be dissolved with warm water before the methanol had any effect on the varnish layer. Further consolidation to weak parts was done after cleaning.

*192. Consolidating paint layer on east wall, HS*

*193. Poor condition of paint layer on east wall (during cleaning), HS*

### 1.3.8 All Walls – Conservation Treatment

**Varnishing –** The appearance of the various wall areas varied slightly after cleaning. The main panel on the west wall was in good condition and the surface had cleaned evenly. Here a single coat of varnish was sufficient. The recessed panel on the west wall and the east wall had been far harder to clean because of damp damage, here two coats of varnish were necessary. One layer was applied before in-painting, followed by a second coat after in-painting.

**Filling of Paint Losses –** Any paint losses to be in-painted were prepared with a marble dust and lime plaster fill (3:1). This could be smoothed with the plastering tool and by rubbing over by hand, and the edges cleaned with a Wishab sponge. No pigment was added to the filling mixture to allow the brilliant white ground to provide transparency to the in-painting.

**In-Painting –** Losses were brought up to a tone below the original using water colours. The choice of colours is limited to the light- and lime-fast range. This was then varnished until the surface was saturated. The colours were then brought up to match the originals using pigments mixed in varnish. The colours were applied in short lines or dots using pure colour to achieve a lively effect and to make it very easy to identify the in-painting from close up (Fig 194). It was found that several applications of varnish had to be made to fills so that they had the same reflection as the surrounding paint surface.

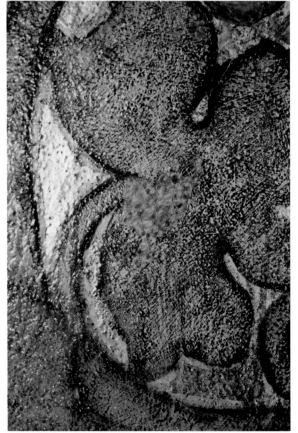

*194. In-painting in dots, HS*

*195. West wall, before conservation, HS*

# APPENDIX 2

# WEST WALL – THE SECOND COMING

Main Wall: The Second Coming (Revelation), union of the human and the divine. (Figs 195, 196)

Pentecost Frieze: Background: Tree of Life (left) and Tree of Knowledge (right) and Judging between the sheep and the goats (Matthew 25:31); Medallions: Left: *'A new heart I will give to you'* (Ezekiel 37:29), Centre: Pentecost (Acts 2:1-4), Right: *'I shall relieve your shoulder of its burden'* (Psalms 81:6).

## 2.1 Pentecost Frieze

### 2.1.1 Condition before Conservation (Figs 197, 198, 199, 200):

**Plaster** – There is a deep settlement crack running up the entire wall from the centre of the doorway arch. The crack divides into two main branches and zig-zags across

the frieze within the central scene that illustrates the Apostles being filled with the Holy Ghost on the day of Pentecost (see Fig 32). The crack must have developed quite shortly after the paintings were completed, and had clearly been filled and retouched in the past, although there are no records of this restoration work. The crack had widened by approximately 1 cm since the first filling was put in, and by a further 2 mm since 1995 when protective facings were applied (see Fig 37). The first filling had broken up and was falling out (Fig 201). Although it was possible to see that the force of the crack had been great enough to break the stones of the walls as well as the weaker plaster joints, the painted plaster is a strong hair mix and even adjacent to the crack it was secure.

Over the rest of the frieze the plaster was sound.

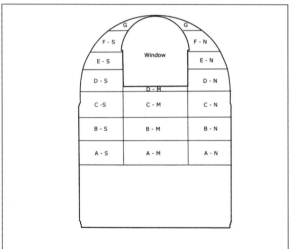

196. *West Wall, diagrams*

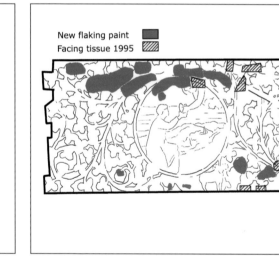

197. *West wall, section AS, condition diagram*

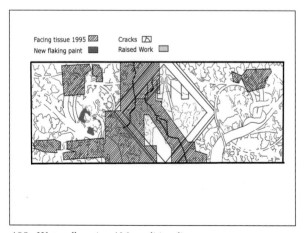

198. *West wall, section AM, condition diagram*

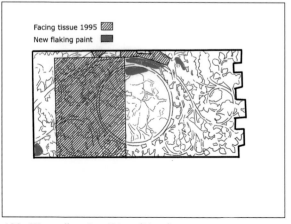

199. *West wall, section AN, condition diagram*

*200. West wall, Pentecost frieze, condition before conservation, HS*

**Paint** – Some mould had developed in the protective facings. There was widespread flaking paint in the vicinity of the string courses, and isolated flaking elsewhere. When retouching the crack the previous restorers had painted over the original paint surface on either side of the crack. The varnish layer had darkened and become mottled.

**Relief and gilded surfaces** – Dirty but in good condition.

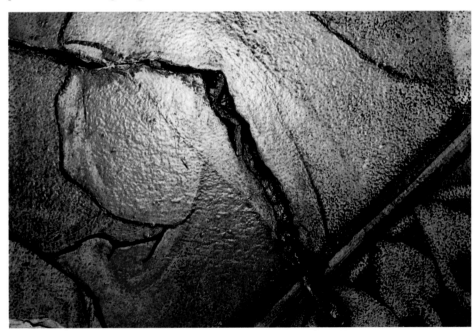

*201. Old filling had broken as crack widened, HS*

### 2.1.2 Conservation Treatment (Figs 202, 203, 204):

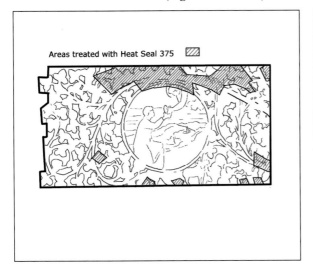

*202. West wall, section AS, treatment diagram*

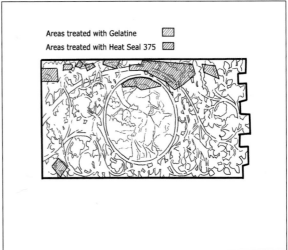

*204. West wall, section AN, treatment diagram*

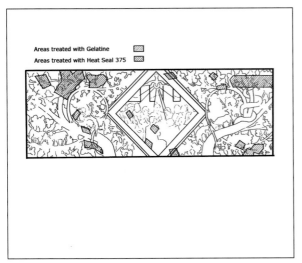

*203. West wall, section AM, treatment diagram*

**Plaster –** The deep crack was cleaned and filled with lime mortar followed by lime:marble powder fine surface filler.

**Paint –** Apart from small trial areas with gelatine, which were only moderately successful, most of the flaking paint was secured with Lascaux Heat Seal 375. Areas where there had been retouching adjacent to the crack required cleaning with poultices of IMS. Elsewhere the painted surface was cleaned with swabs of soap liniment and IMS.

**Relief and gilded surfaces –** All gilded surfaces throughout the decoration were cleaned with tri-ammonium citrate.

**In-painting of losses –** The missing decoration within the crack was recreated over the new filling using water colours followed by pigments mixed with varnish. Minor losses and abrasions adjacent to the crack were in-painted using varnish colours.

This method of in-painting was used throughout the conservation, unless otherwise stated.

In some cases it was possible to refer to the photographs taken by the Royal Commission in 1982 for information about the paintings because much of the damage in the nave post-dated these records. However, the crack across the west wall pre-dated the Commission photographs, and so the paint on the filling had to be re-created on the basis of what survived on either side (Figs 205, 206, compare with Fig 200).

**Varnishing –** All parts of the frieze were given two coats of pure dammar varnish, followed by two coats of matt dammar varnish made by mixing 50cc of wax in 50cc of pure gum turpentine with 400cc dammar varnish. The matt varnish was applied warm.

**N.B.** These varnishes were used for the entire decorative scheme except for the chancel ceiling (see below), and so will not be listed under 'Treatment' for the rest of the report unless the recipe varied.

*205. Pentecost frieze after conservation, SG*

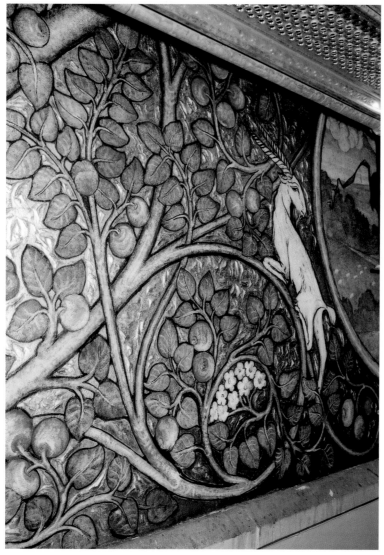

*206. Detail of Pentecost frieze after conservation, HS*

## 2.2 Main Wall Lower Band

### 2.2.1 Condition before Conservation (Figs 207, 208, 209, 210):

*207. West wall, section BS, condition diagram*

*209. West wall, section BN, condition diagram*

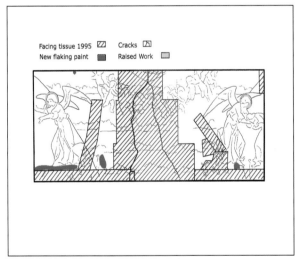

*208. West wall, section BM, condition diagram*

**Plaster –** The deep settlement crack running up from the door to the window passes across the centre of the painting (Fig 211). The crack had caused a shift in the plane of the wall. This shift in plane, and the fact that the stones themselves had cracked (as noted above) had caused a small section of plaster at the base of the wall to become loose. Otherwise the plaster was sound.

**Paint –** Flaking paint was predominantly found along a band above the string course (Fig 212). The flaking had extended beyond the confines of the facing paper applied in 1995 (Fig 213), and in theory there is a danger that this could continue. The paint used in the earlier retouching of the crack was spread over the original paint over quite a wide area on either side of the crack (Fig 214). The surface of the wall was dark and dirty, and this, combined with the dark retouching, obscured the colour difference between the green hillside and the blue sky, making the composition appear quite flat.

*210. Central part of west wall before conservation, HS*

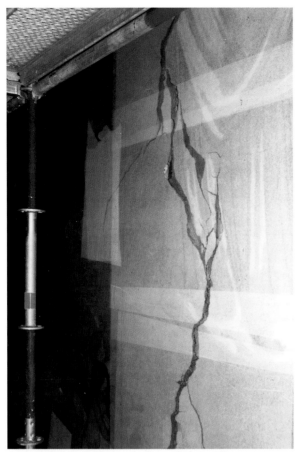

*211.  Settlement crack across the figure of Christ, HS*

*212.  Flaking paint above string course, HS*

*213.  Flaking paint beyond facing paper, HS*

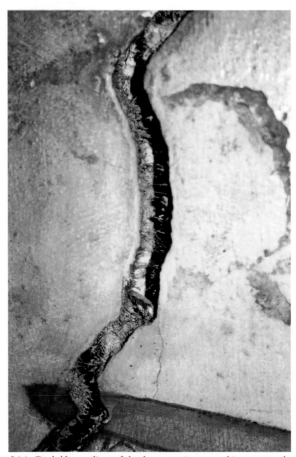

*214.  Dark blue outlines of clouds are previous retouching to conceal the crack, HS*

### 2.2.2 Conservation Treatment (Figs 215, 216, 217):

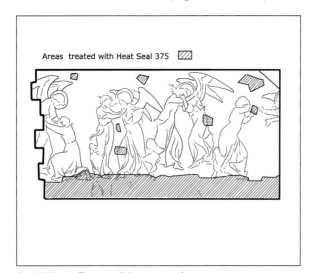

215. West wall, section BS, treatment diagram

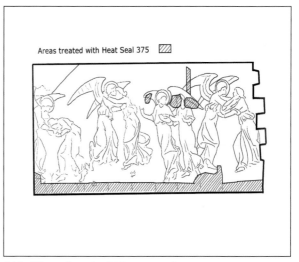

217. West wall, section BN, treatment diagram

216. West wall, section BM, treatment diagram

**Plaster –** The loose fragment of plaster at the base of the crack was re-set using lime mortar (Fig 218). The entire length of the crack was deep filled with lime mortar and surface filled with fine filler (Fig 219).

**Paint –** Weak and flaking paint above the string course was consolidated with Lascaux Heat Seal 375 (Fig 220). Cleaning was with soap liniment and IMS. Previous retouching was removed with poultices of white spirit and IMS, with occasional use of acetone.

**In-painting –** Water colour and varnish colour in-painting was restricted to the crack itself, and areas where paint had been lost due to the effects of damp adjacent to the string course, with some glazing of abrasions on either side of the crack (Fig 221 compare with Fig 219).

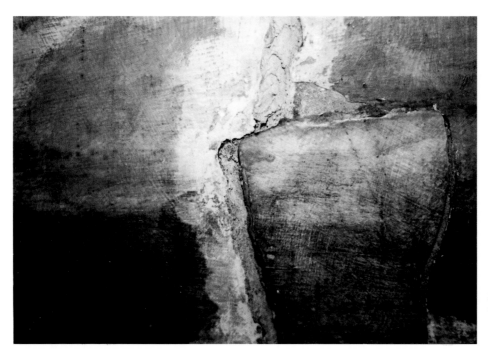

218. Loose section of plaster re-set, the dark over-painting is clearly visible, HS

*219. The filled crack, HS*

*220. Consolidating paint with Lascaux Heat Seal 375, HS*

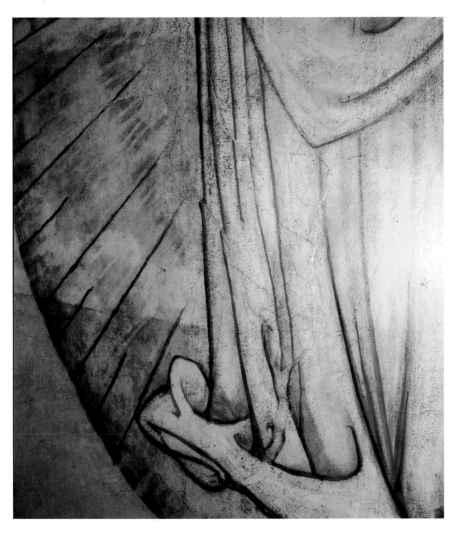

*221. Central crack after in-painting, HS*

## 2.3 Main Wall: Central Band

### 2.3.1 Condition before Conservation (Figs 222, 223, 224, 225):

222. *West wall, section CS, condition diagram*

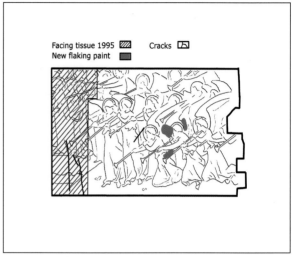

225. *West wall, section CN, condition diagram*

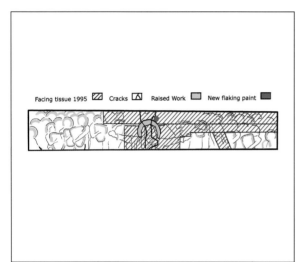

223. *West wall, section DM, condition diagram*

**Plaster –** Generally sound except for the deep central crack and weakness along the base of the wheel window. The crack had caused the surface to shift significantly, affecting the position of the outlines of figures (Fig 226).

**Relief and gilded work –** Much of this had been lost along the base of the wheel window. Elsewhere sound.

**Paint –** Severe flaking and paint loss along the base of the wheel window (Fig 227). Isolated flaking elsewhere.

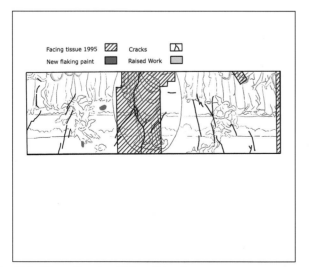

224. *West wall, section CM, condition diagram*

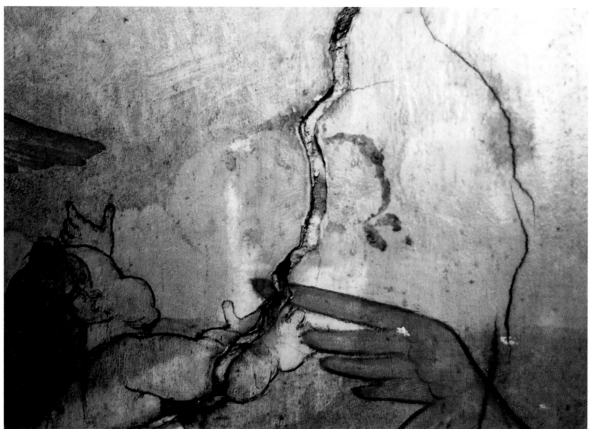

226. *The outline of cherub's hand radically altered by crack, HS*

227. *1995 photograph of damage below wheel window, HS*

### *2.3.2 Conservation Treatment (Figs 228, 229, 230, 231):*

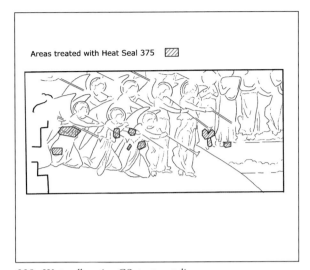

228. *West wall, section CS, treatment diagram*

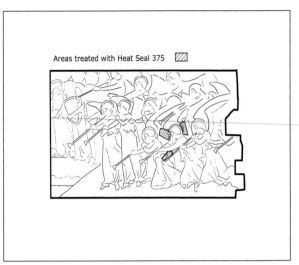

231. *West wall, section CN, treatment diagram*

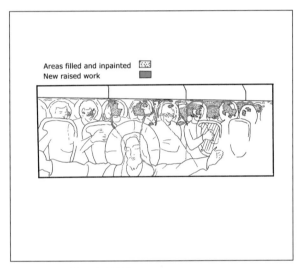

229. *West wall, section DM, treatment*

232. *Building up lost haloes, HS*

**Plaster –** Loose edges along base of window grouted with lime mortar. The deep crack was filled with lime mortar followed by surface filler.

**Relief and gilded work –** Lost areas were built up using gilder's putty (Fig 232). Larger areas of gilding were replaced.

**Paint –** Weak paint was consolidated with Lascaux Heat Seal 375 (see diagram). Stubborn retouching removed with poultices of White Spirit and IMS. Elsewhere, the painting was cleaned with soap liniment and IMS (Fig 233). Some over-painting on Christ's robes was removed with tri-ammonium citrate. Missing sections were in-painted.

230. *West wall, section CM, treatment diagram*

### 2.3.3 Observations:

The profiles of the relief and gilded haloes of the angels immediately beneath the wheel window originally extended over the stone surround of the window. The top edge of the painting at this point would therefore not have been straight (as it is now) but would have followed the curved outlines of the haloes. The shadows of the original outlines may still be seen (see Fig 227).

The position of the Christ figure has been altered so that the hands are not so widely spaced and are set at a slightly different angle (see Fig 70). The outline of the figure itself has also been changed.

The position of one of the relief trumpets has been altered. It is possible to see from this that the artist cut away the plaster surface where the relief work was to be placed (Fig 234).

A red layer may be seen beneath the gilding on parts of this wall (see Fig 64).

*233. Cleaning the surface. The slightly cleaned bands have been cleaned with soap liniment, the central band with IMS, HS*

*234. Incisions in plaster showing changed intention for position of trumpet and figure, HS*

## 2.4 Main Wall: Upper Band

### 2.4.1 Condition before Conservation (Figs 235, 236, 237, 238, 239, 240, 241):

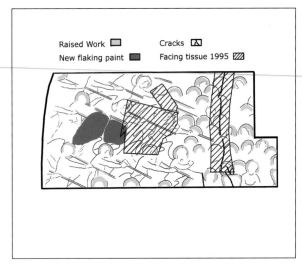

*235. West wall, section DS, condition diagram*

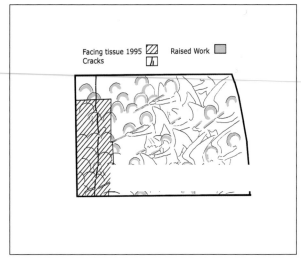

*236. West wall, section DN, condition diagram*

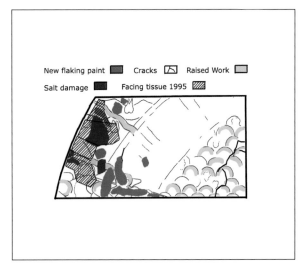

*237. West wall, section ES, condition diagram*

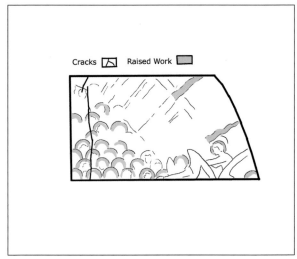

*238. West wall, section EN, condition diagram*

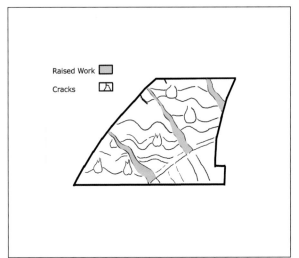

*239. West wall, section FS, condition diagram*

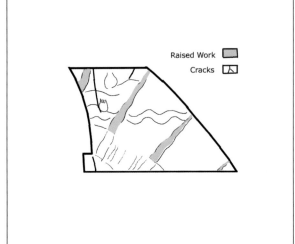

*240. West wall, section FN, condition diagram*

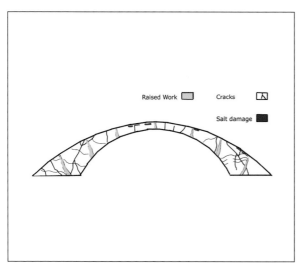

*241. West wall, section G, condition diagram*

**Plaster –** The main settlement crack is reduced to a fairly insignificant width beyond the top of the window. There are several other minor cracks, the plaster was, however, stable.

**Relief and gilded work –** In good condition.

**Paint –** Severe paint loss on the left side above the springing of the arch, with flaking paint and paint loss (Fig 242). The surface of the paint at the apex of the arch had remains of a very thick yellow varnish. Generally the paint was very dirty and dusty (Fig 243).

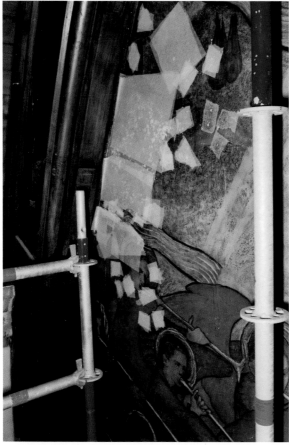

*242. Flaking paint due to salt efflorescence at edge of mural, HS*

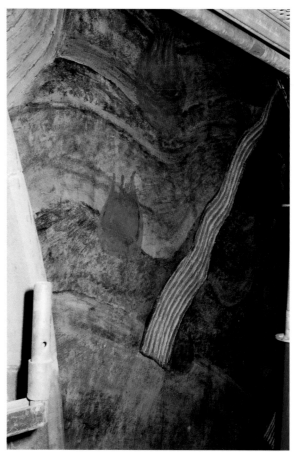

*243. Very dirty surface at top of wall, HS*

### 2.4.2 Conservation Treatment (Figs 244, 245, 246):

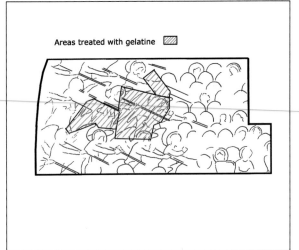

244. *West wall, section DS, treatment*

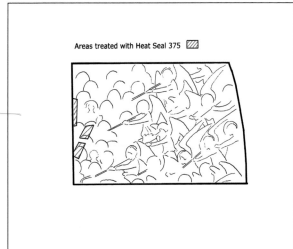

245. *West wall, section DN, treatment*

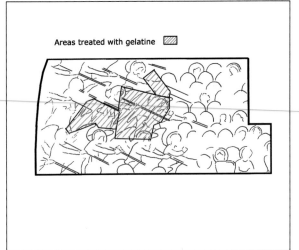

246. *West wall, section ES, treatment*

**Plaster –** All cracks surface filled.

**Paint –** Weak paint was secured with Lascaux Heat Seal 375. Paint losses were filled with fine filler and in-painted.

The yellow varnish was very insoluble. Poulticing with IMS and white spirit softened it slightly, but it could not be cleaned very evenly (Fig 247). Elsewhere the surface was cleaned with soap liniment and IMS (Fig 248).

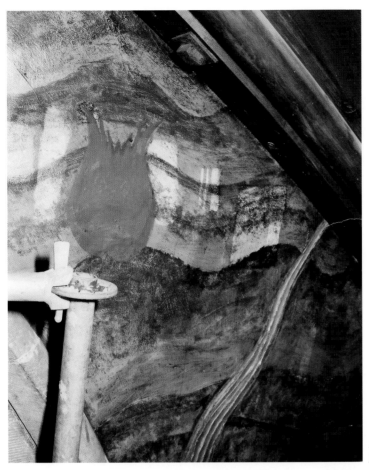

*247. Cleaning trials to remove thick yellow varnish, HS*

*248. The upper part of painting after cleaning, HS*

*249. Chancel arch before conservation, HS*

# APPENDIX 3

# CHANCEL ARCH – THE WORSHIP OF HEAVEN

The Worship of Heaven: from the top: *'great multitude of the redeemed'* (Revelation 7:9) in the *'sea of glass mingled with fire'* (Revelation 15:2); four-and-twenty elders (Revelation 4:4); trumpeting angels; angelic choir; four cherubim representing the four orders of the Catholic Apostolic Church: Apostle in a gold robe holding a crown, Prophet in blue with a harp, Evangelist in scarlet with a Bible and Pastor in white with a staff and lamb, (Revelation 4:6-8) four holy beasts - symbols of the evangelists - Matthew (man), Mark (lion), John (eagle) and Luke (ox). (Figs 249, 250).

## 3.1 Lower Panels – Four Holy Beasts

### 3.1.1 Condition before Conservation (Figs 251, 252, 253):

**Plaster -** There was some slightly hollow-sounding plaster adjacent to the relief work on the left (north) panel (section A). Larger areas of weak plaster were identified on the right (south) panel (section G). The paintings on the lower right (or south) side of the chancel arch are painted on to the joining wall with the chapel, where failing gutters in the valley between the chapel roof and the chancel had caused considerable damp damage to the paintings on both sides of the party wall.

**Relief and gilded work -** This was sound on the left panel. On the right side the relief work had been badly affected by salts. A large section of the ox's halo was missing (see Fig 36), and part of the halo of the eagle had had to be set back in 1993 (Fig 254). The gilding on the eagle's halo was badly damaged (Fig 255).

**Paint -** Damp seeping through from the party wall with the chapel had caused the paint to flake and become detached on the right panel (Fig 256). The paint on the left panel was sound. There was evidence of some retouching on both panels.

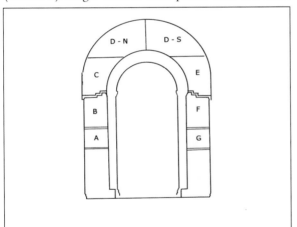

*250. Chancel arch: diagram of sections*

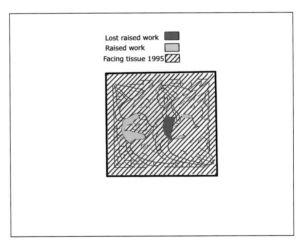

*252. Chancel arch, section G, condition diagram*

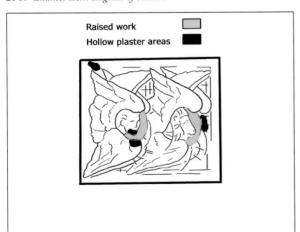

*251. Chancel arch, section A, condition diagram*

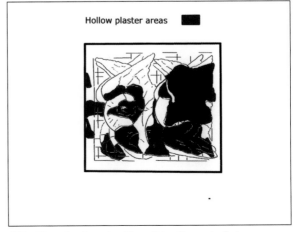

*253. Chancel arch, section G, condition diagram - plaster*

*254. Section of eagle's halo being set back in 1993, HS*

*255. Salt damage to eagle's halo, HS*

*256. Detaching paint, 1995 photograph, HS*

### 3.1.2 Conservation Treatment (Fig 257):

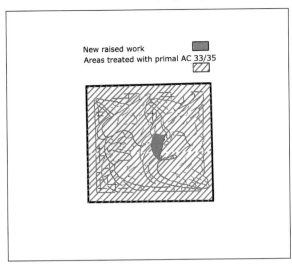

*257. Chancel arch, section G, treatment diagram*

**Plaster** – Loose areas on the right panel were consolidated with Ledan TB1. The hollow-sounding plaster on the left panel was not moving and it was considered best to leave it untreated.

**Relief and gilded work** – The missing halo was built up using gilder's putty bulked up with cotton wool. (Fig 258). All new relief work was regilded and tinted with varnish glazes to match the original (Fig 259).

**Paint** – Flaking paint was consolidated with Primal AC33. The paint surface was cleaned with soap liniment followed by solvent mixtures of IMS and white spirit, often applied in poultices.

### 3.1.3 Observations:

The design of the halo of each of the holy beasts is different. A small fragment of the ox's halo had survived, however, it was necessary to study very early photographs of the chancel arch to see the exact form of the design on the larger missing section (see Fig 27).

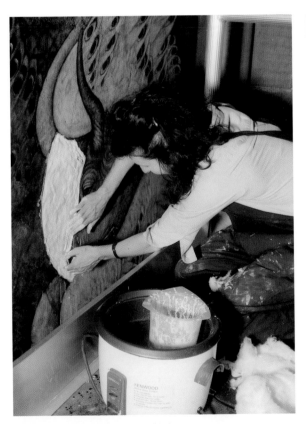

*258. Recreating missing section of halo, HS*

*259. Regilding the new relief, HS*

## 3.2 Four Cherubim

### 3.2.1 Condition before Conservation (Figs 260, 261):

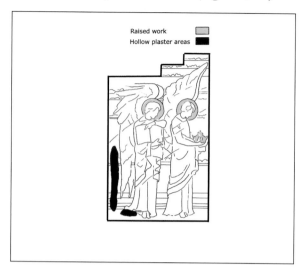

*260. Chancel arch, section B, condition diagram*

*261. Chancel arch, section F, condition diagram*

**Plaster –** Although there were some hollow sounding areas on the left side (section B) the plaster was solid and generally sound. On the lower part of the right hand panel the plaster had broken up slightly due to salt efflorescence (section F).

**Relief and gilded work –** This was in good condition.

**Paint –** The paint on the left (north) side of the arch (section B) was in good condition. That on the right side (section F) had been affected by the damp from the chapel, with paint loss predominantly on the lower half of the panel (Fig 262).

*262. Loose and flaking paint on cherubim, 1995 photograph, HS*

### 3.2.2 Conservation Treatment (Fig 263):

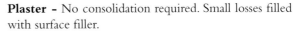

*263. Chancel arch, section F, treatment diagram*

**Plaster –** No consolidation required. Small losses filled with surface filler.

**Relief and gilded work –** This was cleaned with tri-ammonium citrate.

**Paint –** Secured with Primal AC33. Cleaning was slow and difficult and poultices were needed in some places (Fig 264). Areas of paint loss in-painted.

### 3.2.3 Observations:

The artist altered the positioning of the figures in these panels, this is particularly noticeable on the left side (see Fig 105). After the painting had been cleaned it was possible to see the richness of the paint layer (Fig 265).

*264. Starting to clean the painting, HS*

*265. Rich colours of the cleaned cherubim, SG*

## 3.3 Angels and Trumpeting Angels

### 3.3.1 Condition before Conservation (Figs 266, 267):

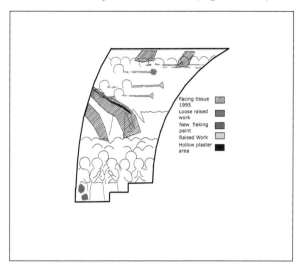

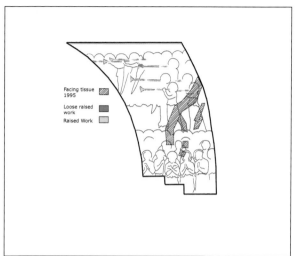

266. *Chancel arch, section C, condition diagram*

267. *Chancel arch, section E, condition diagram*

**Plaster** – The plaster was in good condition except for a small area adjacent to a settlement crack across the left side. Other cracks were superficial.

**Relief and gilded work** – Minor losses and weakness (see diagrams), but generally sound.

**Paint** – Generally sound. Some weakness along the edges of relief work, probably due to shrinking of the gilding size (Fig 268). The paint layer was quite dirty and patchy in places.

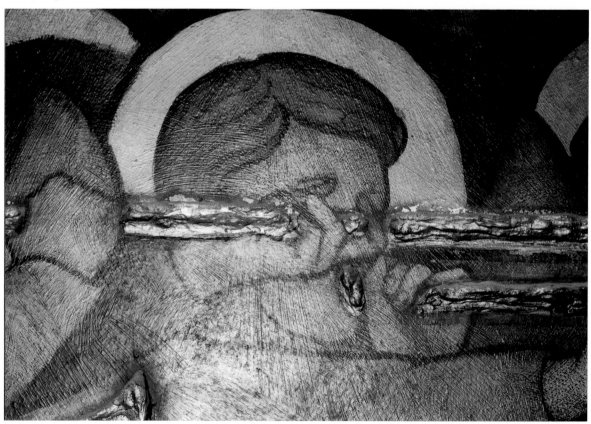

268. *Slight paint loss adjacent to gilding, HS*

### 3.3.2 Conservation Treatment (Fig 269):

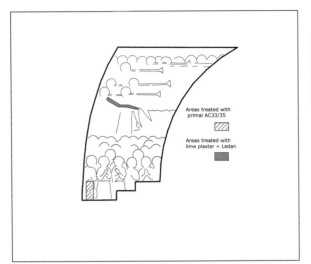

*269. Chancel arch, section C, treatment diagram*

**Plaster** – Ledan TB1 injected to consolidate loose plaster adjacent to crack (section C). Cracks filled with fine filler.

**Relief gilded work** – Missing sections repaired with gilder's putty, and regilded.

**Paint** – Cleaned with soap liniment and IMS; several applications were required because of the amount of dirt (Fig 270). The filling in the crack was in-painted.

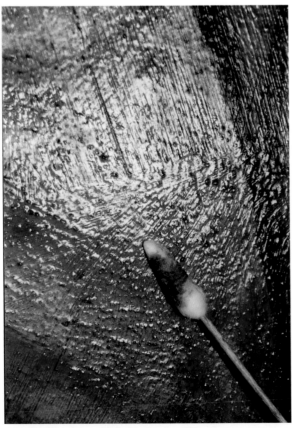

*270. Dirt being removed during cleaning, HS*

## 3.4 Elders and Multitude of the Redeemed

### 3.4.1 Condition before Conservation (Figs 271, 272):

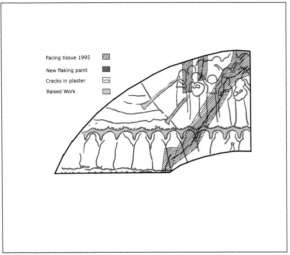

*271. Chancel arch, section DN, condition diagram*

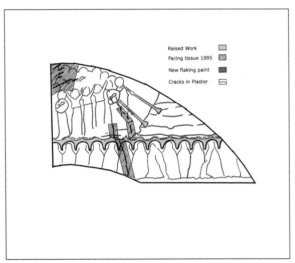

*272. Chancel arch, section DS, condition diagram*

**Plaster** – A significant settlement crack runs across the centre of the panel (Fig 273 and see Fig 275). This appeared to be stable. Otherwise the plaster was sound.

**Relief and gilded work** – The canopy above the seating of the 24 elders is of made of deep relief work (Fig 274). This was generally sound, and well attached to the wall. There were some minor losses of gilding on some of the angels' trumpets.

**Paint** – The paint layer was in good condition, except for minor weaknesses along the top of the relief canopy (Fig 275 and see diagram). The surface was dirty, and some mould growth had developed (Fig 276).

*273. Settlement crack across centre of upper part of chancel arch, HS*

*274. Deep relief work; the coarse surface indicates it contains cotton wool, HS*

*275. Minor losses along top of canopy and dirty surface, HS*

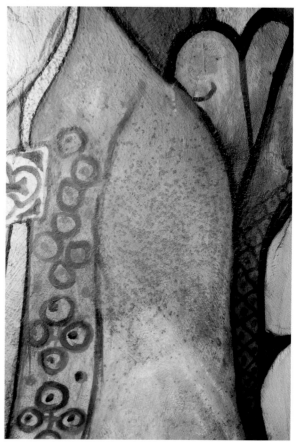

*276. Mould growth on surface, HS*

### *3.4.2 Conservation Treatment (Figs 277, 278):*

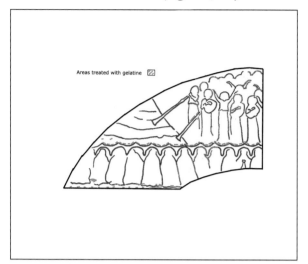

277. *Chancel arch, section DN, treatment diagram*

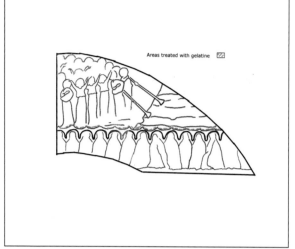

278. *Chancel arch, section DS, treatment diagram*

**Plaster** – Cracks filled with lime mortar followed by fine filler.

**Relief and gilded work** – Any weak edges were consolidated with gelatine. Any surface losses were built up with gilder's putty and re-gilded.

**Paint** – Flaking paint consolidated with gelatine. Surface cleaned with soap liniment followed by IMS.

*279. Working off mobile towers in the nave, HS*

# APPENDIX 4

# NAVE SOUTH WALL – OLD TESTAMENT SCENES

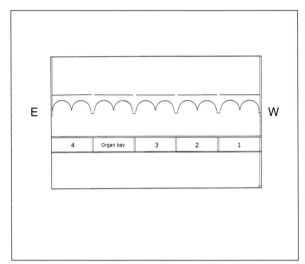

*280. Nave south wall, diagram of panels*

*281. Adam & Eve panel, condition diagram*

Scenes from west to east: Adam and Eve Panel (The Fall): Temptation (Genesis 3:6), Expulsion from Eden (Genesis 3:24), Cain and Abel (Genesis 4:1-8). Noah Panel (Covenant): God's Covenant with Noah (Genesis 8:8-11), Calling of Abraham (Genesis 17:1-8), Sacrifice of Isaac (Genesis 22:1-14). Joseph Panel: Joseph's dreams: sheaves in the fields bowing (Genesis 37:6-7) and sun, moon and stars bowing (Genesis 37:9), Joseph sold into slavery (Genesis 37:23-28), Joseph in slavery in Egypt (Genesis 39:1). The next panel is occupied by the organ case. David Panel: Anointing of David (1 Samuel 16:13), the Ark of the Covenant (2 Samuel 6:3), David charges Solomon with the building of the Temple (1 Chronicles 22:6) (Figs 280).

## 4.1 Adam and Eve Panel

### Scenes – Temptation; Expulsion from Eden; Cain and Abel

#### 4.1.1 Condition before Conservation (Figs 281, 282):

**Plaster –** The condition of the plaster had deteriorated dramatically in recent years (compare figs 282 and 283) particularly in the top left corner of the Cain and Abel scene where it was detached along a band approximately 45cm wide beneath the string course. The plaster surface was badly broken up by salts (Fig 283).

**Paint –** The paint was also in poor condition in the top half of the Cain and Abel scene. The paint had continued to flake after the protective facings had been first applied in 2003 (Fig 284).

*282. Adam & Eve panel, before conservation, 1982 photograph, RCAHMS*

*283. Protective tissue over areas of paint and plaster affected by salts, HS*

*284. Paint flaking beyond facing tissue applied in 2003, HS*

### 4.1.2 Conservation Treatment (Figs 285, 286):

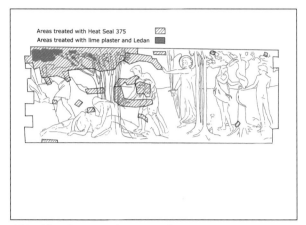

285. Adam & Eve panel, treatment diagram

286. Adam & Eve panel, treatment diagram 2

**Plaster –** Loose plaster consolidated with Ledan TB1.

**Paint –** Additional flaking paint was faced up and all weak and flaking paint was consolidated with Lascaux Heat Seal 375. The paint surface was cleaned with poultices of White Spirit, IMS and Acetone (Fig 287). Losses were in-painted with water colour and varnish paint (Fig 288).

287. Consolidation (left) and cleaning (right) in progress, HS

288. Adam & Eve panel after conservation, SG

## 4.2 Noah Panel

### Scenes – God's Covenant with Noah; The Calling of Abraham; Abraham and Isaac

#### 4.2.1 Condition before Conservation (Fig 289):

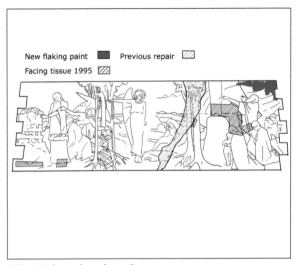

*289. Noah panel, condition diagram*

**Plaster** – There is a large settlement crack across the centre of the scene, where original paint and plaster had been lost over a width of approximately 35-40 cm. The crack runs up from the arch over the door to the string course above the painting and had caused a slight shift in the plane of the plaster surface on either side. The crack had been repaired in the past (unrecorded) with a wide filling which was retouched in oil paint. The surface of the repair did not reflect the light in the same way as the rest of the painting (Fig 290, Fig 33). A second, smaller crack passes across the left side of the painting (the Abraham and Isaac scene). The plaster was slightly detached along the edges of the large repair, but otherwise sound.

**Paint** – There was flaking paint on the top right hand side of the panel (God making his covenant with Noah). Parts of the surface had a fine crackle within the varnish layer (Fig 291). A cleaning trial done in 1993 had resulted in some paint loss (Fig 292).

*291. Flaking paint and surface crackle in the varnish layer, HS*

*290. Detail of previous repair showing difference in paint technique and colour, HS*

*292. 1993 cleaning trial, HS*

### 4.2.2 Conservation Treatment (Fig 293)

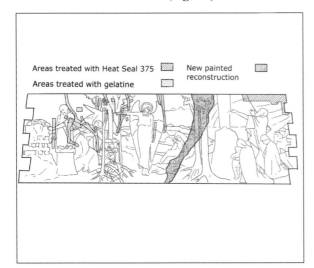

*293. Noah panel, treatment diagram*

*295. Filling prepared with lead white paint, HS*

**Plaster –** The old filling was left in place, but the paint on the surface was removed. The edges of the filling were pared down to reduce the plane difference along the crack. Weaknesses along the edge of the filling were consolidated with Ledan TB1 (Fig 294), and the edges filled with fine filler. The filling was then given several coats of lead white paint as a preparation for retouching (Fig 295).

**Paint –** Weak and flaking paint was consolidated with gelatine. The surface was cleaned. Where the paint was sound and had not been restored it was possible to clean with swabs of soap liniment followed by IMS. More stubborn dirt and over-paints were hard to remove and had to be softened with poultices of IMS and white spirit (Fig 296).

*294. Consolidating the edges of the filling, the previous retouching having been removed, HS*

*296. Poultices softening over-painting, HS*

### 4.2.3 Observations:

There was no evidence for the precise design of the lost part of the painting, because the damage dated from before the first thorough survey of 1982. This meant that the missing section had to be invented with close reference to the original paint remains on either side of the crack. The replacement was done in a combination technique of oil paint in wax paste over the lead white base (Phoebe Anna Traquair's technique), followed by pigments in varnish (Figs 297, 298).

*297. Retouching in progress, HS*

*298. Noah panel, after conservation, SG*

### 4.3 Joseph Panel
**Scenes – Joseph's Dreams; Joseph sold into slavery; Slavery in Egypt (Fig 299)**

*299. Joseph panel, before conservation, 1982 photograph, HS*

### *4.3.1 Condition before Conservation: (Figs 300, 301, 302, 303)*

*300. Joseph panel, condition diagram*

*301. Joseph panel, condition diagram - salt damage*

*302. Joseph panel, condition diagram - plaster*

*303. Joseph panel, condition diagram - paint*

**Plaster –** The plaster was in very poor condition on the left half of the panel. Much of the plaster in the Slavery in Egypt scene was detached, with some areas lost. Most of the surface of this part of the painting was broken up by salt damage. The entire panel was faced up in the 1990s to prevent the paint and plaster from falling off. Over a large area the lower base coat of plaster had completely disintegrated. The skim coat and paint layer were surviving better than the lower plaster, and these two layers, with the facing paper, were 'hanging' independently of the powdery plaster beneath, which had collected as dust in pockets behind the surface, causing the surface to become deformed (Fig 304).

**Paint –** Large areas of paint had been lost between the 1980s and 1990s, particularly from the area where the plaster was detached in the Slavery in Egypt scene – approximately 60% of the paint on this scene was either lost or badly deteriorated. Salt damage also affected the central scene- Joseph sold into Slavery.

*304. Hole in plaster showing cavity behind paint layer, HS*

### 4.3.2 Conservation Treatment: (Figs 305, 306, 307)

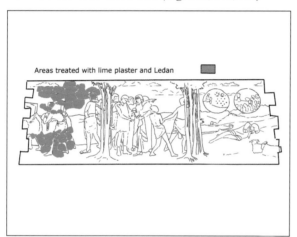

*305. Joseph panel, treatment diagram - plaster*

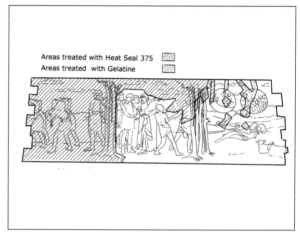

*306. Joseph panel, treatment diagram - paint*

*307. Joseph panel, treatment diagram 2*

**Plaster –** Holes were made in the skim coat where the paint layer was lost. The powdery plaster beneath could be vacuumed out through these holes, and a fresh lime mortar injected behind to fill the void (Fig 308).

**Paint –** The paint layer was consolidated with Lascaux Heat Seal 375 (Fig 309). It was then cleaned with poultices of white spirit, IMS and acetone (Fig 310). Paint and plaster losses were filled with lime mortar followed by lime and marble powder filler (Fig 311). Losses were in-painted using water colours and varnish paints (Figs 312, 313, 314).

### 4.3.3 Observations:

The 1982 RCAHMS photographs (see Fig 299 above) provided extremely useful information about the form of the figures in the badly degraded parts of this panel, since the damage had occurred since they were taken. The photographs were used extensively when in-painting and re-creating missing areas.

*308. Injecting fresh lime mortar, HS*

*309. Rubbing the adhesive into the paint surface, HS*

*310. Cleaning the painting after consolidation, HS*

*311. Painting after consolidation, cleaning and filling ready for in-painting, HS*

*312. Blocking in the lost areas in watercolour, HS*

*313. Building up the tone with varnish paints, HS*

*314. Left side of Joseph panel after conservation, SG*

## 4.4 David Panel

**Scenes – The Anointing of David; The Ark of the Covenant; David charges Solomon with the building of the Temple (Fig 315)**

*315. David panel, before conservation, 1982 photograph, RCAHMS*

### 4.4.1 Condition before Conservation (Fig 316):

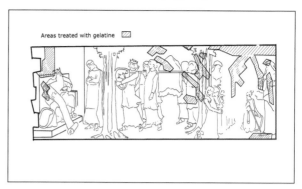

*316. David panel, condition diagram*

**Plaster –** Minor surface cracks, but generally sound.

**Relief and gilded work –** Good.

**Paint –** The surface had a distinct crackle within the varnish layer (Fig 317). There was considerable weak and flaking paint in the top right corner, and the surface was patchy and dirty.

### 4.4.2 Conservation Treatment (Fig 318):

*318. David panel, treatment diagram - paint*

**Plaster –** Surface filling of cracks.

**Relief and gilded work –** Cleaned with tri-ammonium citrate.

**Paint –** Weak paint was consolidated with gelatine. The cleaning of this panel was often slow, requiring poulticing with white spirit and IMS. Limited in-painting and glazing required (Fig 319).

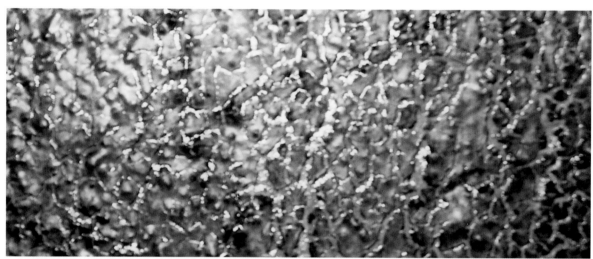

*317. Shrunk varnish layer with paint layer showing behind, HS*

*319. David panel after conservation, SG*

# APPENDIX 5

# NAVE NORTH WALL – NEW TESTAMENT SCENES

320. *Nave north wall, Nativity, Wilderness and Ministry panels, before conservation, 2000 photograph, HS*

321. *Nave north wall, Last Supper and Ascension panels, before conservation, 1995 photograph, HS*

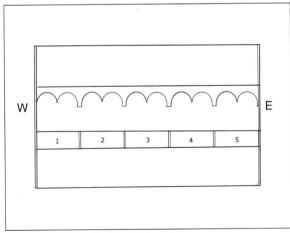

322. *Nave north wall, diagram of panels*

Scenes from west to east: Nativity Panel: Annunciation (Luke 1:26-38), Nativity (Luke 2:6-7), Massacre of the Innocents (Matthew 2:16). Christ in the Wilderness Panel: Baptism of Christ (Matthew 3:13-17), Christ in the Wilderness (Matthew 4:1-12), Calling of the Disciples (Matthew 4:18-22). Ministry Panel: Healing of the Blind (Matthew 20:34), Raising of Jarius's daughter (Luke 8:41-56), Entry into Jerusalem (Matthew 21:8). Last Supper Panel: Last Supper (Matthew 26:17-35), Washing of the Feet (John 13:5), the Betrayal (Matthew 27:49-50). Ascension Panel: Entombment (Matthew 28:59-61), Christ appears to Mary Magdalene (Mark 16:9), Ascension (Mark 16:19) (Figs 320, 321, 322).

Signature:

P A Traquair, 1898, Ascension panel, lower R H corner.

### 5.1 Nativity Panel

### Scenes – Annunciation; Nativity; Massacre of the Innocents

*5.1.1 Condition before Conservation (Figs 323, 324):*

**Plaster –** Surface cracks on left side, otherwise sound.

**Relief and gilded work –** Sound.

**Paint –** Minor isolated areas of detached paint, otherwise sound.

*323. Nativity panel, condition diagram*

*324. Nativity panel, before conservation with facing tissue over cracks and 1995 cleaning trial, HS*

### *5.1.2 Conservation Treatment (Fig 325):*

325. *Nativity panel, treatment diagram - paint*

**Plaster –** Minor cracks surface filled.

**Relief and gilded work –** Cleaned with tri-ammonium citrate (Fig 326).

**Paint –** Cleaned with soap liniment and IMS (Figs 327, 328). Minor glazing required over test area.

### *5.1.3 Observations:*

Slight changes in the positioning of figures by the artist (Fig 329).

326. *Nativity panel, cleaning relief, HS*

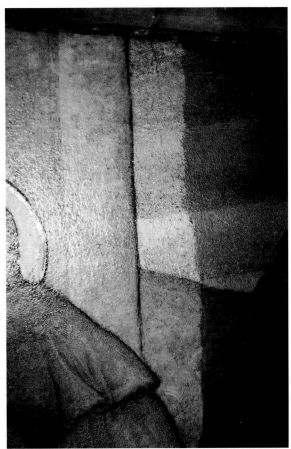

327. *Nativity panel, during cleaning, HS*

328. *Nativity panel after conservation, SG*

329. *Alterations to position of heads, HS*

*330a. Christ in the Wilderness, before conservation, HS*

## 5.2 Christ in the Wilderness

### Scenes – Baptism of Christ; Christ in the Wilderness; The Calling of the Disciples

#### 5.2.1 Condition before Conservation: (Figs 330a, 331):

**Plaster –** Minor surface cracking, otherwise sound.

**Paint –** In good condition, with only minor, isolated paint loss.

#### 5.2.2 Conservation Treatment: (Fig 332):

**Plaster –** Cracks surface filled.

**Paint –** Cleaned with soap liniment and IMS (Fig 332b).

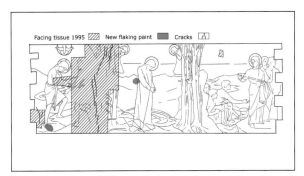

*331. Christ in the Wilderness, condition diagram*

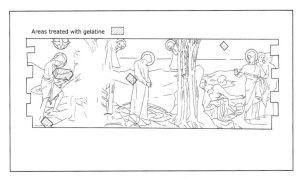

*332. Christ in the Wilderness, treatment diagram - paint*

*332b. Christ in the Wilderness, after conservation, HS*

*333. Ministry panel, before conservation with facing tissue over areas of weak paint, HS*

## 5.3 Ministry Panel

## Scenes – Healing of the Blind; Raising Jarius's Daughter from the Dead; Entry into Jerusalem

### *5.3.1 Condition before Conservation: (Figs 333, 334)*

**Plaster –** Minor surface cracks, generally sound.

**Paint –** The painting was in good condition. There was minor paint loss, mainly along lines of the underlying red line, and minor surface abrasion.

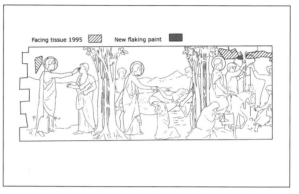

*334. Ministry panel, condition diagram*

### *5.3.2 Conservation Treatment: (Fig 335)*

**Plaster –** None.

**Paint –** Weak paint consolidated with gelatine. Cleaned with soap liniment and IMS (Figs 336, 337a and b).

*335. Ministry panel, treatment diagram - paint*

*336. Cleaning Ministry panel, HS*

132

*337a.Ministry panel during cleaning, HS*

## 5.4 Last Supper

### Scenes – Last Supper; Washing of the Feet; The Betrayal

#### 5.4.1 Condition before Conservation: (Fig 338)

*338.  Last Supper, condition diagram*

**Plaster –** Minor surface cracks. The surface of the right hand side of the panel was badly broken up and pitted by salts, however, the plaster had not become detached.

**Paint –** Severe paint loss due to salt damage on the right side of the panel (the Betrayal scene). The right side of the panel had been faced up in 1995, and the paint had continued to flake since then.

#### 5.4.2 Conservation Treatment: (Figs 339, 340)

*339.  Last Supper, treatment diagram - paint*

*340.  Last Supper, treatment diagram 2*

*337b.  Ministry panel after conservation, SG*

**Plaster –** Surface cracks and losses filled.

**Paint –** The facings applied in 1995 had been put on in several layers. These were reduced to a single layer as much as possible to ease application of the adhesive (Fig 341), and the paint was consolidated using Lascaux Heat Seal 375 (Fig 342). The painting was cleaned with poultices of white spirit, IMS and acetone (Fig 343, 344).

Losses were built up using fine filler. The fillings were in-painted using water colour and varnish paint glazes (Fig 345).

### 5.4.3 Observations:

The glass in Christ's hands had originally been a small ewer (Fig 346).

*341. Salt-damaged paint visible through thinned tissue layer, HS*

*342. Consolidation in progress, HS*

*343. Cleaning in progress, HS*

*344. The Betrayal after consolidation and cleaning and before filling and retouching, HS*

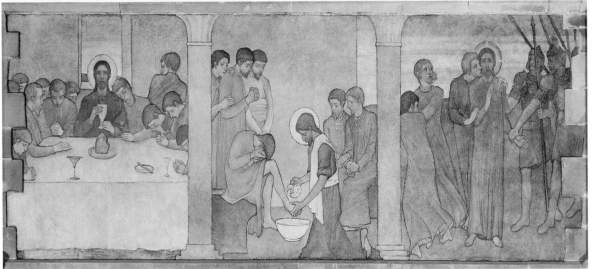

*345. Last Supper panel after conservation, SG*

*346. Shadow of ewer visible beneath drinking glass, HS*

## 5.5 Ascension Panel

### Scenes: The Entombment; Christ appears to Mary Magdalene; The Ascension

### 5.5.1 Condition before Conservation: (Figs 347, 348, 349)

*348. Ascension panel, condition diagram - salt damage*

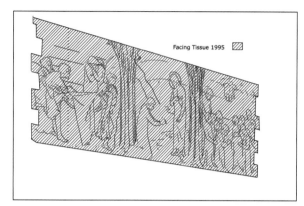

*347. Ascension panel, condition diagram*

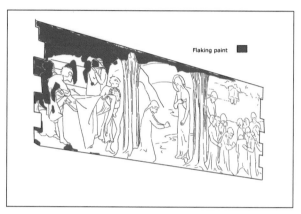

*349. Ascension panel, condition diagram - paint*

**Plaster –** The surface was pitted and broken by salts on the left hand side of the panel (the Entombment scene). This damage corresponds to the damage on the Betrayal scene which is on the other side of the engaged column. Both scenes had been affected by damp entering because of a faulty down pipe against the wall outside. The plaster had not become detached.

**Paint –** The paint had flaked very badly particularly on the left side of the panel (Fig 350, taken before applying facing paper in 1995), and the entire panel had been faced up in 1995 (see Fig 321).

*350. Damage caused by damp, 1993 photograph, HS*

### 5.5.2 Conservation Treatment: (Figs 351, 352)

**Plaster –** Surface cracks and losses filled with fine filler.

**Paint –** weak paint was consolidated using Lascaux Heat Seal 375. The painting was cleaned with great difficulty using poultices of white spirit, acetone and IMS. Losses in the paint layer were filled with fine filler and in-painted using water colours (Fig 353) followed by varnish paint glazes (Fig 354).

*351. Ascension panel, treatment diagram - paint*

*352. Ascension panel, treatment diagram 2*

*353. In-painting in progress, HS*

*354. Ascension panel after conservation, SG*

355. *Spandrel panels, 2000 photograph, SG*

# APPENDIX 6

# NAVE CLERESTORY – SPANDREL PANELS

Some very decayed fragments survived above the clerestory windows in the first two bays from the chancel arch on the south wall – the east bay and the organ bay (Fig 355).

## 6.1 East Bay

### 6.1.1 Condition before Conservation

All that survived in the first bay from the east (adjacent to the chancel arch) were small sections in the narrow wall space between the windows (Fig 356) and between the window and the chancel arch. The decoration is a relief lattice or trellis pattern. The fragments in this bay had been faced up during previous inspections of the painting in 1993, therefore the paint layer could not be seen. The missing plaster above these fragments had been replaced at some stage, and roughly painted so as not to appear blank from the ground.

The small amount of surviving plaster was sound and adhering well to the wall. Although the surface had had a protective facing over it for several years, the paint seemed to be in good condition.

During repairs to the plaster in the spandrel panels in 2002, the plasterers had spread a skim over the facing tissue (Fig 357).

### 6.1.2 Conservation Treatment

The overlying plaster skim and the facing tissue were removed with warm water. The exposed plaster edge was edge pointed with a lime mortar. The surface was lightly cleaned with IMS. The fragments were given a single coat of dammar varnish (see Fig 123).

*356. Fragments in east bay, 1995 photograph, HS*

*357. Removing plaster skim, HS*

### 6.2 Organ Bay

About six or seven fragments of various sizes had survived in this bay. For the most part they were concentrated along the top of the wall, although three extended down to meet the top of the window (Fig 358).

Much of the paint was missing but on one or two fragments enough survived to make out some of the design, which appears to be a procession of figures with relief work along the top. This conforms with the evidence from early photographs. The relief is decorated in both silver and gold leaf (Fig 359).

Unlike the east bay, the painted remains in this bay were not faced up on previous occasions because they were inaccessible from the available scaffolding.

#### 6.2.1  Condition before Conservation

**Plaster –** In places the plaster was so powdery that it crumbled away if touched, and mounds of sandy broken plaster deposits had collected on the stone surrounds over the windows and at the base of the spandrels between the windows. The plaster had separated from the wall over large areas (see Fig 49).

**Priming layer –** Where it survived, the white priming was adhering well to the rough-cast for the most part, but its surface had broken into widespread blistering due to salt efflorescence.

**Paint –** The paint had broken up and was obscured over much of the surface by salt deposits. In places the paint between the deposits was quite sound, but there were also widespread areas of flaking paint.

#### 6.2.2  Conservation Treatment

**Plaster –** Very loose fragments with little or no surviving paint were removed. Those surviving fragments with more paint remains that could be safely left *in situ* were edge-pointed using lime mortar (see Fig 50). The edges were further consolidated with lime slurry. Surrounding plaster remains were brushed off and the surface was re-plastered (see Fig 124).

**Paint –** The paint layer was consolidated using gelatine. Because of its poor state the surface could only be lightly cleaned. No in-painting was undertaken. The painted fragments were then given two protective coats of gloss varnish.

*358. Fragments in organ bay before conservation, HS*

*359. Silver and gold leaf relief work with outlines of processing figures, HS*

*360. North aisle, ceiling, west and north walls before conservation, SG*

# APPENDIX 7

# NORTH AISLE
# THE PARABLE OF THE WISE & FOOLISH VIRGINS

(Continued)

Continuation of the Parable of the Wise and Foolish Virgins (Matthew 25:1-3): wise virgins continue their journey and foolish virgins turn back, union of human with divine spirits, foolish virgins arrive too late. Vignettes providing commentary: (above) Angel teaching children, *'Mercy and Truth are met together, Righteousness and Peace have kissed'*, angels and mortals kneel before the Divine Child held by His Mother, Angel weeps, (below) *'He that will follow me, let him take up his cross and walk'* (Matthew 16:24), The Eucharist with kneeling spirit. West wall: Angel comforts a foolish virgin; above, two angels *'put thou my tears into thy bottle'* (Psalm 56:8), and, over arch into nave, Christ knocks at the door of the soul (interpretation of *The Light of the World* by William Holman Hunt).

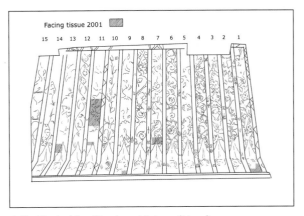

*362. North aisle ceiling, bays 15-1, condition diagram*

## 7.1 Ceiling

### 7.1.1 Condition before Conservation: (Figs 360, 361, 362)

**Timber –** The timber joists of the ceiling had been affected by dry rot at the western end of the ceiling adjacent to the party wall with the north side of the nave (Fig 363). The laths of the plaster 'bays' had also been badly affected by rot in this corner. The weakness of this part of the ceiling became manifestly obvious when roofing repairs were being carried out as part of the conservation of the building in 2001/2, and a piece of the painted lath-and-plaster in the westernmost bay collapsed when pressure was put on it (Figs 364, 365 and see Fig 45). The construction of the ceiling is surprisingly flimsy, and the back of the painted plaster surface is very close to the sarking boards of the roof. Elsewhere the timber joists appeared to be sound. The condition of the lathwork over the rest of the ceiling was not known, but assuming that the timbers are kept dry, it should be sound.

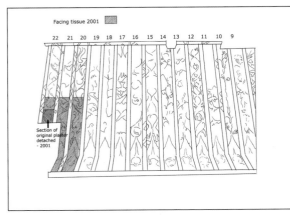

*361. North aisle ceiling, bays 22-9, condition diagram*

*363. Timber affected by rot, HS*

*364. Fragment of ceiling dislodged during roof repairs, HS*

*365. Hole in ceiling, HS*

**Plaster –** The plaster was in good condition.

**Paint –** Apart from slight flaking paint on the timbers affected by rot at the west end of the ceiling, the paint on the joists was in good condition. The paint on the plaster bays was generally sound, again with the exception of the two westernmost bays where damp had caused some flaking. Losses had occurred along the joins between the plaster bays and the wooden joists (Fig 366). In addition to the small section of painted plaster that collapsed, some minor damage was caused during repairs to the roof when nails used to secure the sarking boards broke through to the painted surface (see Fig 46).

*366. Flaking paint caused by damp and losses along weak joint between lath-and-plaster and joist, HS*

### 7.1.2 Conservation Treatment: (Figs 367, 368)

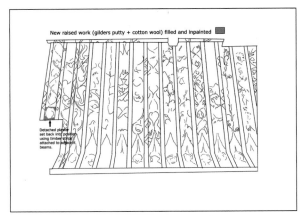

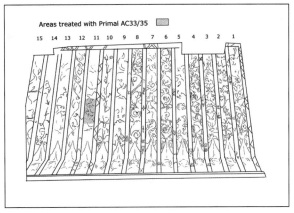

367. *North aisle ceiling, bays 22-9, treatment diagram*

368. *North aisle ceiling, bays 15-1, treatment diagram*

**Timber –** During the building contract the two rotten joists at the western end had reinforcing metal plates set in with resin from above, and new timber edging to maintain their structural function. This meant that the profile of the hidden part of the joists was wider than the original. In order to be able to slot back the section of plaster that had fallen down it was necessary to cut some of the resin and new timber away, otherwise there would have been insufficient space for the repaired section.

**Plaster –** During treatment of the fragment of painted plaster that had been dislodged, the rotten laths were removed from the back, and loose plaster was pared down to a smooth base (Fig 369). A muslin scrim was attached to the plaster with lime casein to strengthen it and replacement balsa wood laths were glued to the back of the fragment (Fig 370). The repaired plaster fragment was set back in place and supported on thin timber strips screwed to the timber joists (Fig 371), which also hold in place the adjacent weakened plaster which had been pushed out of plane (Fig 372).

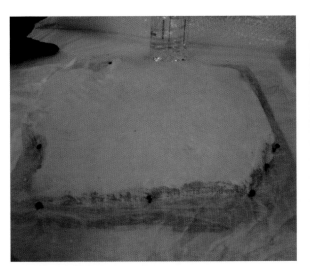

369. *The back of the fallen fragment during treatment, HS*

370. *The back of the fallen fragment with muslin scrim and balsa wood strips, HS*

*371. Timber strip attached to joist with fragment set back, HS*

*372. Fragment with losses filled and in-painting in progress, HS*

**Paint** – A protective facing tissue had been applied to the weak joins between the plaster bays and timber joists where the paint was vulnerable (see Fig 47). These were removed and the weak paint secured using a lime slurry. Flaking paint was consolidated with gelatine. Small losses were filled with lime mortar followed by surface filler. The surface was cleaned using soap liniment and IMS (Fig 373). Some in-painting was required to complete missing sections around the fragment that had been re-instated and the wooden battens supporting the fragment of ceiling plaster were painted to match the surrounding decoration (Fig 374). Elsewhere on the ceiling very little in-painting was required, and this was done with water colours and varnish paint (Fig 375).

*373. Cleaning in progress; the losses along the joints have been filled, HS*

*374. Replaced fragment after conservation, HS*

*375. Ceiling after conservation, SG*

*376. North aisle north and east walls before conservation, SG*

## 7.2 Walls (Fig 376)

### 7.2.1 Condition before Conservation: (Figs 377, 378, 379, 380, 381, 382, 383, 384, 385, 386, 387, 388, 389, 390)

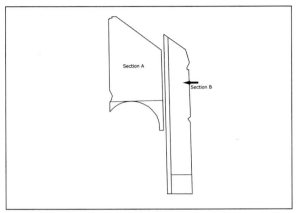

*377. North aisle, west wall, diagram of sections*

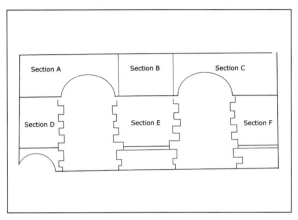

*378. North aisle, north wall, diagram of sections*

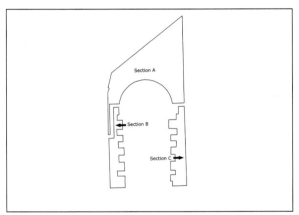

*379. North aisle, east wall, diagram of sections*

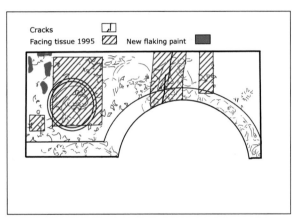

*380. North aisle, north wall, section A, condition diagram*

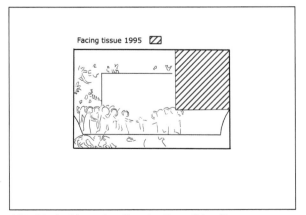

*381. North aisle, north wall, section B, condition diagram*

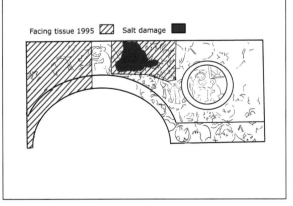

*382. North aisle, north wall, section C, condition diagram*

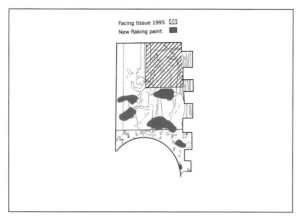

*383. North aisle, north wall, section D, condition diagram*

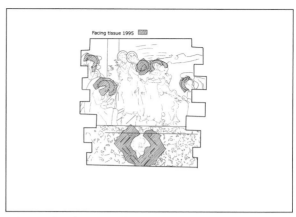

*384. North aisle, north wall, section E, condition diagram*

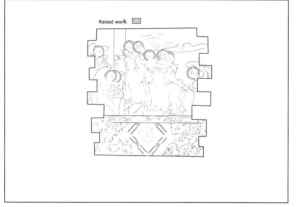

*385. North aisle, north wall, section E, condition diagram 2*

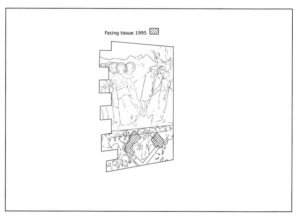

*386. North aisle, north wall, section F, condition diagram*

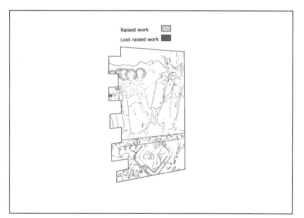

*387. North aisle, north wall, section F, condition diagram 2*

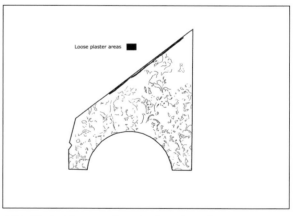

*388. North aisle, east wall, section A, condition diagram*

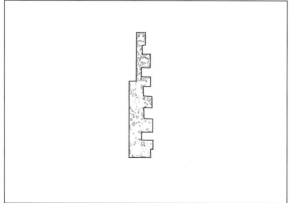

*389. North aisle, east wall, section B, condition diagram*

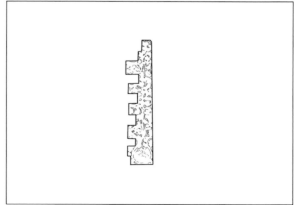

*390. North aisle, east wall, section C, condition diagram*

*391.  Settlement crack and adjacent paint loss, 1995 photograph, HS*

*392.  Previous retouching within areas of flaking and lost paint, HS*

**Plaster –** Deep settlement cracks over both windows had caused the joints between the stones around the windows to widen noticeably (Fig 391). Damp had penetrated at these points and caused salt efflorescence which had broken up the plaster surface. There is retouching (date unknown) applied directly to the plaster exposed by paint loss (Fig 392). Damp entering along the wall head had also caused some salt efflorescence. The plaster had become slightly detached along the crack above the right hand (easterly) window, but elsewhere it was sound.

**Relief and gilded work –** The paste used in the N aisle is very brittle and had shrunk and curled away from the surface quite badly. A few small pieces had been lost (Fig 393). Protective facings had been applied by HSCC staff in 1995 (Fig 394).

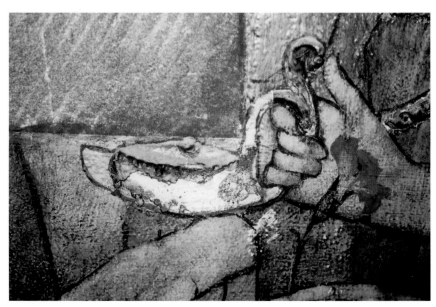

*393.  Brittle and detached relief work, HS*

*394. North aisle, north wall before conservation, SG*

**Paint –** Where damp had penetrated through the walls the paint had been badly affected by salts. This was noticeable in the lower left corner (western end) of the north wall where the surface was quite pitted. Damp had caused the paint to flake off in patches over an area above the right hand window (see Fig 391). An area of very yellow varnish was noted at the top of the west wall of the chapel, reminiscent of that found at the top of the great west wall (Fig 395). Elsewhere the paint was sound, but the varnish had darkened considerably. During inspection visits made in the 1990s HSCC staff had applied protective facing tissue and had carried out some large cleaning trials (see Fig 394).

*395. Yellow varnish at top of north wall, HS*

## 7.2.2 Conservation Treatment: (Figs 396, 397, 398, 399, 400, 401, 402)

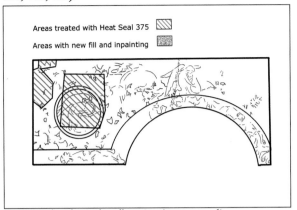

396. *North aisle, north wall, section A, treatment diagram*

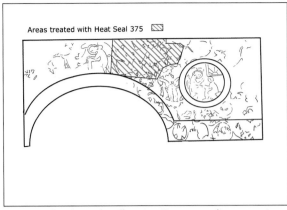

397. *North aisle, north wall, section C, treatment diagram - paint*

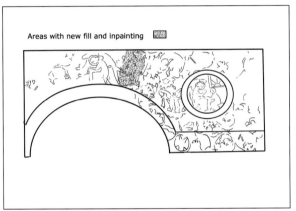

398. *North aisle, north wall, section C, treatment diagram 2*

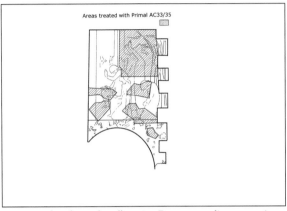

399. *North aisle, north wall, section D, treatment diagram - paint*

400. *North aisle, north wall, section E, treatment diagram*

401. *North aisle, north wall, section F, treatment diagram*

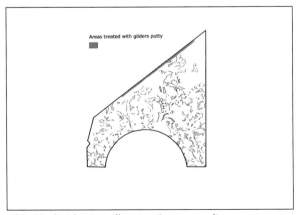

402. *North aisle, east wall, section A, treatment diagram*

**Plaster** – Any loose plaster was consolidated with Ledan TB1. Cracks were filled with lime mortar followed by fine filler.

**Relief and gilded work** – Because the relief work was so brittle it was not possible to lay it flat. Gilder's putty was packed behind loose sections and losses were filled and re-gilded (Fig 403).

**Paint** – Weak or flaking paint was consolidated with gelatine (Fig 404). The very yellow varnish on the west wall was removed by poulticing with acetone and white spirit and then rubbing off the softened varnish (Fig 405). Other areas that had required fixing were cleaned with IMS poultices. Elsewhere the paint was cleaned with soap liniment and IMS, and any necessary in-painting carried out (Fig 406). The plain wall above the arcade between the north aisle and main chancel was redecorated.

### 7.2.3 Observations:

The original lighting of this chapel was similar to that in the south aisle – two pendant lamps hanging from the centre of each of the two arches through to the chancel. Any other light would have come from oil lamps. The chapel, like the rest of the building, would therefore have had quite low lighting.

*404. Flaking paint after consolidation, HS*

*403. Replacing lost relief work, HS*

*405. Area of darkened varnish during cleaning, HS*

*406.  North aisle after conservation, SG*

407. *Detached band of decorative paper, HS*

408. *Flaking paint, HS*

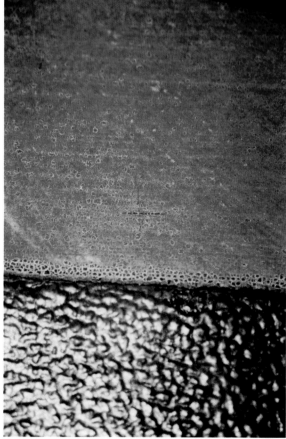

409. *Shrinking of paint. A mark for placing the stencil design is visible, HS*

410. *Reattaching loose paint with gelatine applied through tissue, HS*

156

# APPENDIX 8

# CHANCEL CEILING

## 8.1 Chancel Ceiling

### 8.1.1 Condition before Conservation:

**Wood –** The ceiling is painted onto wood, which was in good condition. The joints between boards had widened slightly.

**Paper –** Bands of a thick decorative paper had been attached to the wooden boards using tacks, and possibly glue. The paper had split in places and become a little buckled and detached (Fig 407).

**Paint –** The paint layer was generally quite sound, there was, however, some fairly isolated flaking (Fig 408). The paint layer had shrunk in places due to the shrinkage of the original size coating (Fig 409). It was also dirty and in places there were smears as if the ceiling had been cleaned before.

### 8.1.2 Conservation Treatment:

**Wood –** None.

**Paint –** Weak paint was re-attached using gelatine (Fig 410). The paint surface was cleaned with 5% sodium carbonate solution in warm water (Fig 409 and see Fig 97). This will have removed most of the size coating previously applied to protect the paint. Minor losses were in-painted in varnish colours. The plain end wall was redecorated.

**Varnish –** The entire surface was given a single coat of matt varnish (see Fig 17).

### 8.1.3 Observations:

Pencil crosses indicating the placing of the stencil cards may be seen in several places (see Fig 409). A box of stencil pins was found behind the crenellated moulding, along with paper cigarette packets and matchboxes. These have been left *in situ.*

*411. Cleaning in progress, HS*

412. Baldacchino, SG

# APPENDIX 9

# CONSERVATION OF OTHER ARTWORKS

## 9.1 Baldacchino

The baldacchino is a fixed, vaulted canopy supported by four Corinthian columns which originally stood over the altar (since removed) in the apse of the chancel. It is constructed of sandstone, plaster, and iron, and is decorated with red and blue paint, gold leaf, mosaics and sculpture (Fig 412). The mosaics represent the three aspects of the Holy Trinity: Father (Alpha and Omega – south), Son (Lamb – west) and Holy Spirit (Dove – north). Originally there were three sculptures of angels on the gables. Only two survive – on the west and north; one with a gilded harp, the other with gilded cymbals. The two sculptures in the alcoves represent St Paul and St Peter. An empty gable plinth and two further alcoves on the east, less visible, side of the structure are capable of displaying sculptures, but it is not clear if any were ever made or installed.

### 9.1.1 Condition before Conservation

There was evidence of crude blue, red and gold over-paint on the decorated bands around the arches and the three mosaics (Figs 413, 414). Some plaster ornaments were detached or missing, and the surface was covered with a thick layer of dirt and dust. Blue-grey paint on the underside of the cupola appeared to cover an original sky-blue paint layer. The blue-grey over-paint was actively flaking and areas of loss had been in-painted.

### 9.1.2 Conservation Treatment

Dust was removed from the surface of the structure with soft hair brushes and a vacuum cleaner. The gilding and mosaics were cleaned with tri-ammonium citrate (2.5% in water), cleared with cold water (Fig 415). The undecorated east face of the baldacchino was difficult to access and could not easily be cleaned.

*413. Crude blue and gold over-paint, HS*

*414. Crude red over-paint, HS*

159

415. *Effect of cleaning gilding, HS*

Some pieces of gilded plaster decoration were recovered from the recesses of the canopy, but not reattached, as it was not clear where they belonged. They have been retained *in situ*. Some loose plasterwork in the upper part was re-attached using an equal mixture of lime putty, sand and Ledan, TBI. This mixture was also used to re-attach three small obelisks at the back of the Baldacchino. In the lower part, loose plasterwork was re-attached, where possible, with a two part epoxy adhesive, as the Ledan/sand/lime-putty mixture, used during conservation work of the upper part, had proved ineffective.

The flaking blue-grey paint on the underside of the cupola appeared to be painted on top of (possibly original) sky-blue paint, confirmed by a small exposure window (Fig 416). The underside of the cupola was repainted using a colour that matched what was believed to be the original scheme.

416. *Small exposure window to show earlier paint layers, HS*

### 9.1.3 Laboratory analysis

Samples were taken to record the number and order of paint layers prior to redecoration and examined under an optical microscope:

Sample 1 (from underside of cupola): A blue paint layer could be seen over a more greenish-coloured paint. No dirt layer was visible between the two, suggesting a short time between applications.

Sample 2 (paint flake from actively flaking area near apex of cupola): the external blue-grey paint layer had become separated from the underlying paint (a dark gap was clearly visible). It seemed that lean, bright-blue paint was over the blue-green base paint layer in this area.

Sample 3 (from decorative area under arch) (Fig 417) revealed what appears to be carefully-applied gold leaf (rather than paint), overlying extremely crudely-applied, ultramarine-blue paint. It was unclear when this decoration was carried out, but it seemed highly unlikely to be original. No previous paint layers were evident between this polychrome decoration and the substrate. The stonework in this area was probably intended to be bare.

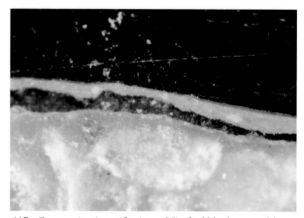

417. *Cross-section (magnification x 25) of gold lead over crudely applied blue paint, HS*

## 9.2 Stained Glass

The stained glass in the chancel clerestory, chapel and north aisle is by Hardman Studios of Birmingham (Bibl 2).

East window of the chapel: The Transfigured Christ flanked by Moses and Elijah with, below, Peter, John and James, (1848, lengthened 1876).

South wall of the chapel: The Lost Piece of Silver and The Lost Sheep, (1878).

Chancel clerestory: south-east: The Blessing of Children, Mary and the Box of Ointment and The Widow's Mite (1877), north east: The Marriage at Cana, The Raising of Jarius's Daughter and The Healing of the Blind Man (1877), north: Our Lord teaching out of Peter's Boat, The Miraculous Draft of Fishes and The Sermon on the Mount, (1878).

North aisle: north wall (right) Nicodemus with Our Lord at Night, The Good Samaritan, Nathaniel brought to Our Lord by Philip (1878); east wall: The Pharisee and the Publican, and The Prodigal Son and The Syrophenicean Woman (1878).

The wheel window in the nave is reported in The Scotsman in 1885 to be by Ballantine: 'The great wheel window in the west gable, high up over the porch, has a diameter of 20 feet, it has a centre quatrefoil with six radiating lights, which have been filled with stained glass by Ballantine' (Bibl 3).

All windows were conserved by Christian Shaw during the building contract. His method was as follows: Good quality colour photographs were taken of the windows before their removal. After the windows were removed; templates of the windows were made. Rubbings and good quality colour photographs were taken of the windows in the studio before the windows were dismantled. Each piece of glass was cleaned, and broken or damaged glass repaired. The windows were releaded using the rubbings as a guide for the positioning of the lead lines. The Lead

was soldered and sealed using linseed oil putty. The panels were brushed and cleaned. Copper ties were added as appropriate and outer leads fitted to suit final sizes. Before being fitted back in place, the window grooves were cleaned and brushed. The windows were re-set, tie bars placed, copper ties tightened, wooden chalks fitted into tie bar mortices to hold the windows firm while the windows were pointed.

## 9.3 Ten Commandments

In the basement on an internal wall beneath the east end of the nave was a canvas with the Ten Commandments painted in oil paint. The artist and date are unknown, but stylistically it appears to pre-date the building. The canvas was glued straight on to the wall. As the internal wall was to be demolished, the canvas was given a protective facing applied with Lascaux Heat Seal 375 and removed. The canvas was conserved, remounted on a honeycomb laminate hardboard, restored and revarnished. The canvas was given a new oak frame and rehung in a circulation space within the offices (Fig 418, 419).

418    Canvas of the Ten Commandments relocated in circulation space, SG

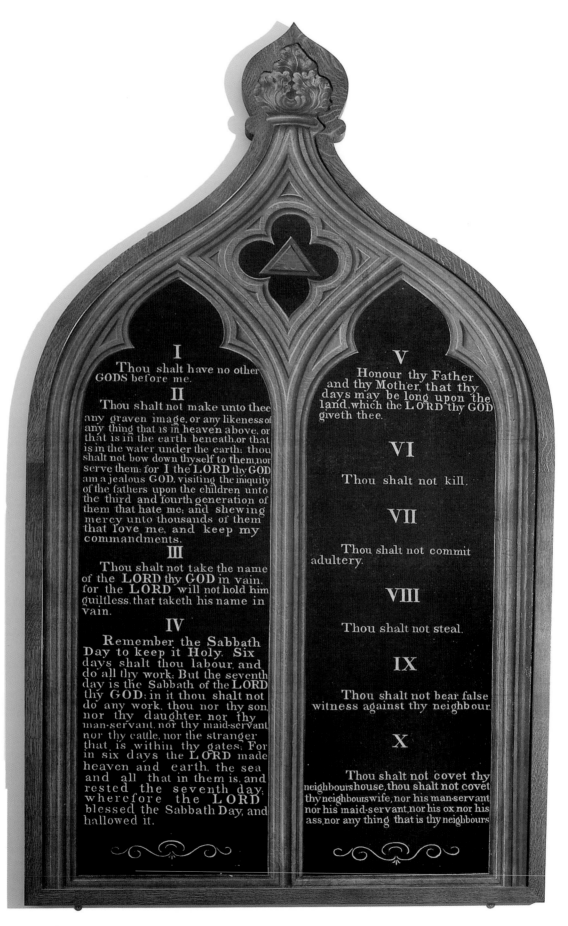

*419. Canvas of the Ten Commandments, SG*

# REFERENCES & BIBLIOGRAPHY

**References in text:**

1. Margaret L Macdonald, *Studio Talk*, The Studio, Vol 12, 1898, pp189-190

2. *Hardman Catalogue of Windows* Birmingham Central Library

3. *The Catholic Apostolic Church*, Broughton Street, The Scotsman, 31 October 1885, p8

4. Communication from Dr Sally Rush to Kate Love, 2006.

5. Letter from Dr R F Stevenson to Linda Fleming, 1983

6. Morris, A F, *A Versatile Art Worker: Mrs Traquair*, The Studio, Vol 34, 1905, pp339-340

7. Letters from Phoebe Anna Traquair to William Moss, National Library of Scotland

8. *Mural Decoration for Churches*, Journal of Decorative Art, September 1901 p 241

9. F. Morley-Fletcher, *Wall decoration*, RIBAS 1910 Vol 17

**Unpublished Reports and Documents:**

Dr F R Stevenson, October 1979, Bellevue Reformed Baptist Church - Historical Note

Elizabeth Cumming, 1986, *Phoebe Traquair and her contribution to Arts and Crafts in Edinburgh*, Edinburgh University Thesis

John Sanders, June 1988, Heriot-Watt History Seminar Paper on the Catholic Apostolic Church

Historic Scotland, 1984 & 1988, Architect's Reports,

Simpson & Brown, 1990, Architect's Inspection Report

Linda Fleming, 1993, HSCC Conservation Report

Ray Hemmett, 1995, HSCC Conservation Report

Fiona Allardyce, 1999, HSCC Conservation Report

Linda Fleming, HSCC Environmental Monitoring Reports, 03.03.99–31.08.99

David Hyde Consultants, April 1999, Timber Survey Report

Apex Property Care, Environmental reports, April 2001 – December 2005

Fiona Allardyce, 2002, HSCC Supplementary reports: Nave Clerestory and North Aisle

Construction Materials Consultants, Infrared Survey reports 1 (December 2002), 2 (March 2003), 3 (December 2004)

Fiona Allardyce, 2004, HSCC Interim Conservation Report, Phase 1 – South Aisle (Chapel)

Fiona Allardyce, 2006, HSCC Conservation Report, Phase 2

**Published Documents**

*A Guide to the Mural Paintings*, 1900, Catholic Apostolic Church, Edinburgh

Sam McKinstry, 1991, *Robert Rowand Anderson, Premier Architect of Scotland*, Edinburgh University Press

Columba Graham Flegg, 1992, *Gathered Under Apostles, A Study of the Catholic Apostolic Church*, Clarendon Press, Oxford

Elizabeth Cumming, 1993, *Phoebe Anna Traquair 1852-1936*, National Galleries of Scotland

Cumming, Sanders, Flegg, et al, 1993, *Phoebe Anna Traquair* Centenary Exhibition Catalogue, Edinburgh

Hannah Eastwood, *The Analysis of Pigments and Plasters*, UKIC Postprints of British Museum Conference 1997.

Elizabeth Cumming, *Phoebe Anna Traquair 1852-1936*, National Galleries of Scotland, 2005

164